Acclaim for *The Adderall Diaries*

"If you're the type of reader who always wants to know what to expect, Stephen Elliott isn't your guy. But if you can take your literary sharp turns without hitting the brakes—or knowing exactly where you'll end up—you won't find a more provocative, masterful, thrilling ride than this."

—Meredith Maran, *The San Francisco Chronicle*

"The book's most affecting passages are unlike anything being written today. They manage to fuse the radical subjectivity of the individual struggling to understand himself with a tender bafflement at the psychological evasions of modern life in America."

—Steve Almond, *The Boston Globe*

"Stephen Elliott's superb, sprawling meta-memoir might be just what the genre needs. . . . [It] is at once skittish and deeply focused: In a single rotund paragraph, Elliott can ping-pong between webcam sex, financial anxiety, hypothetical affairs with college students and murder confessions."

—Scott Indrisek, *Time Out New York*

"*The Adderall Diaries* is neither a Kerouac-like brag, nor an 'Oprah'-ready record of suffering and recovery. Rather, it is its own weird hybrid, a painfully honest and meticulously crafted memoir wrapped around a true-crime story that gets to the very essence of its time and place."   —Scott Timberg, *The Los Angeles Times*

"A book that begins as a true-crime tale of a murder trial and becomes a searing, self-conscious memoir of drug addiction, obsession and art as a means of survival. . . . Powerful and unusual."

—Craig Morgan Teicher, *Minneapolis Star-Tribune*

"Ambitious and emotional and brilliantly orchestrated, an embroidery of memoir and true-crime reportage that's so stunning that I can't imagine Elliott writing about the above-mentioned murder case without also confronting his past (or vice versa). . . . Each strand is insightful and lucid; woven together, they form a thriving work of art." —Michael Miller, *Fanzine*

"The intensity of Elliott's often beautiful prose evokes the effects of Adderall, the attention deficit medication. Yet the book shows a concern for order . . . [B]eneath these devices throbs an all-pervasive sense of the elusiveness of truth. Memories deceive, and almost everyone in this book—including the author—is a fantasist." —Juliet Wittman, *The Washington Post*

"Though it sidesteps traditional memoir elements of revelation, redemption, and closure, it affords both reader and author something much more valuable: a transcendent inquiry into the nature of the self." —Sean Nelson, *The Seattle Stranger*

"*The Adderall Diaries*, a brutally open-eyed memoir about growing up surrounded by violence, clad in the scattered threads of Capote-style crime reporting, is a strange beautiful thing." —Chris Michel, *The Brooklyn Rail*

"A daring and riveting memoir of acute observation and astringent honesty. . . . Inspired by the blood-dark lyricism of Norman Mailer and Truman Capote, Elliott not only pieces together chilling (his 'urge to be hurt and humiliated') and mordantly funny (his dot-com interlude) stories from his rough, boldly improvised life, he also ponders the enigmas of Sylvia Plath and Paris Hilton and shrewdly reports on the murder trial of a mad-genius computer programmer. . . . Elliott is a poet of pain." —Donna Seaman, *Booklist* (starred review)

"An endlessly fascinating memoir by a profoundly courageous writer. . . . Despite the luridness of the subject matter, the author creates a refined, beautiful work of art. . . . Deserves a place on the shelf next to such classics of uninhibited American introspection as *On the Road* and *A Fan's Notes*."

—*Kirkus* (starred review)

"You don't just read *The Adderall Diaries*; you fall right into them. You read as if you are a few words behind the writer, trying to catch up, to find out what happens, to yell at him that he's doing a great job. And he is. It's a brilliant book."   —Roddy Doyle

"Stephen Elliott is one of those 'people who keep searching when everything is dark'—I don't know a more hauntingly fearless writer, and this is an immediate, visceral, and ultimately beautiful book."   —Nick Flynn

"I felt like a voyeur reading Stephen Elliott's memoir—what is shocking and unbearable to most of us is commonplace to him. . . . Reading *The Adderall Diaries* is like taking a step toward the edge of a cliff so you can peer down and imagine what it might be like to slip and fall. Normally we shudder and step back. Stephen Elliott jumps, and his harrowing, riveting memoir convinces you to follow him vicariously."   —Amy Tan

"*The Adderall Diaries* is a startling and original concoction, an irresistible melding of reportage and memoir and reconstruction. This is Stephen Elliott's best book, perfectly suited to his gifts as a seeker, as a storyteller, as a poet of wounds, unwelcome and otherwise."   —Sam Lipsyte

THE ADDERALL DIARIES

ALSO BY STEPHEN ELLIOTT

Novels

*Happy Baby**
What It Means to Love You
A Life Without Consequences
*Jones Inn***

Erotica

My Girlfriend Comes to the City and Beats Me Up

Nonfiction

Looking Forward to It#

As Editor

Where to Invade Next
Sex for America
Stumbling and Raging: More Politically Inspired Fiction
Politically Inspired: Fiction for Our Time

---

* This is my best novel. You should read this one first.

** This is my first book and I don't recommend it. I was twenty-one when I wrote most of it and the publisher, a good friend operating on a small budget, misspelled my name on every other page.

\# This is a diary of the 2004 presidential campaign. Due to deadlines, the footnotes are in the back, as endnotes, and the narrative ends at the Democratic Convention, instead of the election, which some readers find unsatisfying. It's my only funny book.

THE ADDERALL DIARIES

A Memoir

Stephen Elliott

Graywolf Press

Photo/Illustration Credits
Chapter 1: View from Window, by Justin St. Germain. Chapter 3: Vietnamese Girl Fleeing in Terror after a Napalm Attack, by Nick Ut. Still from Hans and Nina's Wedding Video. Chapter 7: Paul Hora in Court, by Vicki Behringer. Beverly Palmer, by Norman Quebedeau. Chapter 9: Ramone Reiser, by Norman Quebedeau. Prosecution Puzzles, by District Attorney Paul Hora. Still from Hans and Nina's Wedding Video. All other photos by the author or Anonymous.

This publication is made possible by funding provided in part by a grant from the Minnesota State Arts Board, through an appropriation by the Minnesota State Legislature, a grant from the National Endowment for the Arts, and private funders. Significant support has also been provided by Target; the McKnight Foundation; and other generous contributions from foundations, corporations, and individuals. To these organizations and individuals we offer our heartfelt thanks.

NATIONAL ENDOWMENT FOR THE ARTS

MINNESOTA STATE ARTS BOARD

WELLS FARGO

Published by Graywolf Press
250 Third Avenue North, Suite 600
Minneapolis, Minnesota 55401

www.graywolfpress.org

Published in the United States of America

Cloth ISBN: 978-1-55597-538-8
Paperback ISBN: 978-1-55597-570-8

2 4 6 8 9 7 5 3 1

Library of Congress Control Number: 2010922922

Cover design: Rodrigo Corral

Those blessed structures, plot and rhyme—
why are they no help to me now
I want to make
something imagined, not recalled?
I hear the noise of my own voice:
The painter's vision is not a lens,
it trembles to caress the light.
But sometimes everything I write
with the threadbare art of my eye
seems a snapshot,
lurid, rapid, garish, grouped,
heightened from life,
yet paralyzed by fact.
All's misalliance.
Yet why not say what happened?
Pray for the grace of accuracy
Vermeer gave to the sun's illumination
stealing like the tide across a map
to his girl solid with yearning.
We are poor passing facts,
warned by that to give
each figure in the photograph
his living name.

—Robert Lowell, "Epilogue"

CONTENTS

This is a work of nonfiction. Situations may have appeared in other works in different forms and significantly different context. Characters are not conflated. Events are sometimes presented out of sequence but timelines are not intentionally altered. Many names and details have been changed to protect identities. Much is based on my own memories and is faithful to my recollections, but only a fool mistakes memory for fact.

THE ADDERALL DIARIES

PROLOGUE

My father may have killed a man.

It was 1970, the year before I was born. The year the United States invaded Cambodia and the voting age was lowered to eighteen. He was thirty-five, the same age I am now, living in his parents' house with my mother and one-year-old sister on the north side of Chicago, trying to make it as a writer.

They lived across from a park, a large park for a city block but not a green park. Chicago ran on a system of patronage with Richard J. Daley, the kingmaker, at the top of the pyramid. It was a crooked town, and proud of it. Someone got paid off with a contract and covered the park in cement, a swingset, and a baseball diamond, turning it into a hard place filled with rocks.

The neighborhood was changing. Older residents, mainly immigrants who had arrived following the First World War, were moving to the suburbs. The new people were from Tennessee and other points south. They had less money and more children. They were louder, or at least that's how it seemed, especially to longtime tenants like my dad, who wasn't doing so well financially himself.

He was at work on a book about euthanasia and retirement homes, an idea given to him by an editor at a large publishing house. He wrote on the sunporch, constantly distracted by the sound rattling through the screens. It was almost Independence Day and the explosions had been going off all week. Occasionally he clenched his teeth and let out a yell that my mother and grandmother ignored. The anger was part of the package. To love my father you had to accept the outbursts, wait for them to pass, and move on to the next thing. It was something he had been doing since he was a child when his mother would tell the other siblings not to challenge him. "Your brother's nervous," she would say. Anyone who stays with my father over time has come to this basic fact.

On the Fourth of July he sat on the front steps with his neighbors, a crippled man and his wife, watching the park, cursing the firecrackers blowing off all around them. The neighbors pointed to a couple of boys right across the street. My father stood in the afternoon sunshine. He wasn't happy with the way his book was going. He wanted to impress the neighbor, and anyway he'd had enough. It was hot and humid, a concrete swamp. He gave no warning. He grabbed one of the boys, searching his pockets, taking whatever stuff he had. The boy said something smart and my father smacked him across the mouth. The boy was thirteen, fourteen years old.

In the evening my father walked to the corner drugstore to buy the Sunday paper. It had gotten cooler and he walked slowly past a gang of teenagers, friends of the boy he'd hit earlier. The boys said a few words under their breath and my father ignored them. Returning through the park, he stopped at the fountain to take a drink.

A man called out, "Did you hit my kid?" The man was drunk, barefoot, striding diagonally across the park. Two men followed behind at a distance, eager to see what would happen. The streetlights were on and the fireflies were blinking. My father didn't run; he just stood there.

The man punched my father and my father didn't fight back.

The house was just across the street but he made no move to run and get up the stairs. He was paralyzed. Seeing there was no danger, the two friends joined in. The three men hit my father from all sides, his eyes swelling, his mouth bleeding. But he never went down. He stood, holding his newspaper, getting punched in the face.

The men walked away, laughing, and for some reason my father followed. They looked back at him and told him to fuck off. They didn't want to go home; they didn't want my father to know where they lived. And then a police car pulled to the curb and the men were arrested.

My father pressed charges but nothing happened. He hired an attorney and they tried to bribe an official with $500 to get the charges raised to aggravated assault. But their attempt failed in court and my father lost what little faith he had in the institutions that are supposed to protect us and provide justice. Or maybe it was a faith he never had. He'd lived in Chicago virtually all his life and knew how the game was played. This was his neighborhood and he had been humiliated on his own block. His doctor told him he was as close to having a concussion as a man could be without actually having one. He told himself he would never again doubt his ability to take a punch.

There are pictures of my father from that summer in 1970, his shirt covered in blood, giant bruises fading from black to purple around his eyes, wearing sunglasses and without. I've seen the pictures, or I remember seeing them. I don't always trust my own memory. He talked about the beating to me, my sister, my uncle. It loomed over him, hovered around his shoulders like a coat he couldn't get out of. He never talked about the rest.

My father's writing career never really took off. His hardcovers weren't released in paperback. I got the impression he was too concerned with what editors wanted and how much he was getting paid per hour, which is death for a writer. He told me he didn't believe in rewriting. He penned two pulp novels populated with characters averse to exploring their own motivations. He also wrote pornographic books, some of which he republished under other names. They lined his office shelves with titles like *Visiting Aunt* and *Sin Safari*. One of his favorite stories involved telling a woman he wrote pornography and her responding, "You write pornography? I live pornography!" He also published a book-length interview with Al Capone's piano player called *My Years with Capone*. Except it wasn't actually Al Capone's piano player, it was Al Capone's lawyer, and at the last minute the lawyer backed out. The interview was the best book my father ever did, but it was a lie, like a lot of other things.

My father got out of writing and into real estate. When I was eight my mother was diagnosed with multiple sclerosis, confining her to the living room couch for most of the next five years. She died when I was thirteen and I ran away from home a month or two later. After a year sleeping on the streets, I was taken into custody by the state and spent four years in various state-sponsored institutions. My father made money, married someone with a good job, moved to the suburbs, and had new children. My little brother and sister went to private schools.

In 2001 my father sent me his memoir along with a box of correspondence and an unfinished novel. I was living in a studio next to a transient hotel and across from a chocolate factory. The prison bus stopped down the street and the crack whores crossed back and forth in front of the factory, breaking into the dumpster after hours and digging out mangled boxes of toffee. That Christmas Eve a man tried to jump in my window from the building across the echo chamber. He missed and fell three stories to the ground and broke his leg.

I had just published my first hardcover novel, *A Life Without Consequences*, set in the group homes where I spent my adolescence. My father clearly hoped that I would write about him. There was no other explanation for sending me his correspondence. He had three children in Chicago he could have given it to.

When I was young he used to give me books to read about strong, silent men who did the right thing and didn't care what anybody else thought. They were criminals and soldiers who never backed down from anything. They were tough and lived according to a simple, unspoken moral code. "That's your dad," my father would tell me.

According to the memoir, after he was beat up, the children in the neighborhood mocked him and his friends abandoned him. He felt spooked, unsafe, like he could get "made." His masculinity shattered, he moved with my mother and sister to a small, furnished rental on the North Shore where he bought a shotgun and practiced shooting in the woods behind the house. Or he says he did. All I have is what people tell me and what they write down.

A year had passed since he was beat up. By then he was done with his euthanasia book and doing work in a rehab, counseling drug addicts and having an affair with one of the junkies, which would cost him his job. He sawed off the barrels of the gun. When he fired toward the trees there was just a puff of smoke. He bored holes in the gun so he could run a belt through it and bought a raincoat and tried strapping the gun inside the arm using the belt over his shoulder. He knew the work schedule of the man who had beaten him. Barry Kling promised to get the police patrol schedules outside the man's house, but he never did.

In his memoir my father refers to the man as Jerk Number One and the two men that joined in as Jerk Number Two and Jerk Number Three. He wrote, *"I set up a check list of procedures.*

"Unfortunately wearing the long coat over the sawed-off shotgun was impractical now, in the heart of Chicago's warm July summer. Even the mornings were warm. I could still do it, but people would notice it and it would look peculiar. And the mornings were bright.

Jerk Number One came out to his station wagon about 7:30 AM, the sun had already been up quite a while. I'd be visible like nobody's business.

"Still it had to be now, as I was leaving the country. Then the case would die a natural death.

"I had a black vinyl hat to wear. I could put on a false beard and mustache, and eyeglasses with no glass in them. I was nervous but determined.

"Jerk Number One was killed one morning while sitting in his car. Apparently someone got out of a car behind and across the street from his and put both barrels of a sawed-off 12-gauge shotgun through the side window on the driver's side." He finished the section with this strange caveat: *"If any state's attorney or Chicago policeman is reading this, I am stating categorically that I had nothing to do with Jerk One's death. I suppose he must have had other enemies besides myself."*

Shortly after that my parents moved to England where I was born.

I stayed home from work sick as I read through the entire manuscript. His denial was typical, with its hope to take credit and claim innocence at the same time. I didn't doubt he killed that man. It fit everything I thought I knew about my father: driven by pride, anger, and violence. Especially pride. The most startling detail was not the murder, but the lack of remorse for the child who grew up without his father as a result of my father's actions. The boy is never again mentioned in the text. I wanted to meet him. I imagined getting to know him, going to bars together and drinking Budweiser, and one day saying, "My father killed your father." He would be around fifty now. I looked for information everywhere but I came up against a dead end. I combed through microfiche of Chicago newspapers from the time. I hired students to help me with research. I went to the neighborhood looking for long-term residents who might remember something. I contacted the Chicago Bar Association trying to find the attorney who had represented my father and they told me he was deceased.

The University of Michigan did a study on murders committed in Chicago in the 1970s. There was no white man shot with a shotgun, sitting in his car.

I've been holding on to that information for a long time. Wondering where it fit.

BOOK 1

Preliminary Motions

CHAPTER 1

May; Golden State; Suicidal Thoughts; A Year without Speed; Floyd Mayweather Comes Up Short; "Your Guy Just Confessed to Eight Murders"; Lissette; The Part about Josie

It's May 4, 2007, the morning after the Golden State Warriors won the first round of the NBA playoffs against a Dallas team that was supposed to be one of the best ever to play the game. I'm not thinking about murder confessions.

I'm taking Adderall, a Schedule D amphetamine salt combo, emptying the time-release capsules into glasses of orange juice, trying to break down the casings surrounding the amphetamines to see if I can get all the speed at once. I swirl the juice, press against the beads with the back of a spoon. I take five milligrams at eight, five more at noon. My roommate is gone. He left his door open and his computer sitting on the floor and I shuttle back and forth between his room, where I pass hours playing cards online, and my room, where I stare out the window and struggle to write something and then give up and go back to his room and play some more cards. It's a lonely, pointless existence, but that's what happens.

I head to a party at a small publishing house in the Mission. All the kids are there, eating cake and bean dip and drinking beer. It's 5:00 and they're off work. One girl wears bright red pants that come to her rib cage. She's just back from Germany and says everybody in Europe is wearing these kinds of pants.

I talk with Doug and Brent about the Warriors' run, how they barely even made the play-offs.

"I have the Chicago Bulls DVDs at home," Doug says. "I watch the games of the nineties over and over again. It helps me relax. You know the best player on that team wasn't Michael Jordan? It was Scottie Pippen. Scottie could dunk from the free-throw line at any time. He just elevated, and it was done."

I know what he's talking about. I lived in Chicago all those years. I remember the play-offs against New York, Scottie Pippen flying into Patrick Ewing like a warhead destroying a mountain. Of course it was Jordan, and to a lesser extent Phil Jackson, who enabled Pippen to do what he did. He was never any good after he left the Bulls. He had his payoff, his championship rings, his millions, the rest no one will ever know.

I feel ready to kill myself.

After the party I stop at the café. There's a girl from the writing program there, one of the new fellows. She's young, with bright red cheeks and a mop of healthy brown hair. She says she had been somewhere and heard someone say my name. She says it bitterly.

"I'm famous," I say. "Which is why I have so much money. Women follow me everywhere." But I'm joking. I don't have any money. I've had writer's block for almost two years.

I go home and start drinking. By midnight it's done. I'm asleep on the couch, beneath an eight-panel collage my ex-girlfriend Lissette made for me. She made it while she was still living with her husband in a little house on the other side of the Bay, before our relationship broke apart her marriage. Each panel is two feet high and eighteen inches wide and comprised mostly of fetish models cut from mainstream magazines: women in gas masks, men on operating tables stuck full of hypodermic needles. Glossy pictures glued on black cardboard, peeling at the edges. It's the only decoration I have. The collage brought us back together for a while but in the end it was the unfinished work of a child, an accurate description of us both.

I have two roommates who won't be coming home. We live in a large, cheap apartment in the outer Mission with strange gray carpet and a view of the water reclamation plant on a hill nearby. So instead of going to my room, I fall asleep on the couch and then eventually go downstairs where I toss and dream until morning when I wake up feeling scratchy but fine and I take ten milligrams of Adderall and hope I can do this without doing it again.

My psychiatrist lives just down the street from me. I can walk there. I see her once a month, or once every three months, and she prescribes my pills. The pills make me crazy, I know that, but I don't see the alternative. It's really just speed, no different from the original amphetamine salts Gordon Alles injected in June 1929, and almost identical to the Pervitin used by German paratroopers in World War II as they dropped behind enemy lines in a state the British newspapers described as "heavily drugged, fearless, and berserk." It's the same stuff injected in high doses in the Haight Ashbury that Allen Ginsberg was talking about in 1965 when he said, *"Speed is anti-social, paranoid making, it's a drag, bad for your body, bad for your mind."*[1]

Without the Adderall I have a hard time following through on a thought. My mind is like a man pacing between the kitchen and the living room, always planning something in one room then leaving as soon as he arrives in the other. Adderall is a compound of four amphetamine salts. The salts, with their diverse half lives, metabolize at different rates, so the amphetamine uptake is smoother and the come down lighter. And I wonder if I'm not still walking back and forth in my head, just faster, so fast it's as if I'm not walking at all.

My psychiatrist is tall and thin and her skin hangs loosely around her face. I like her quite a bit although I've never spent more than fifteen minutes with her. She works from her home and the door to a small waiting room is always open on the side of her house. There are magazines there, in particular *ADD Magazine*. The magazine is full of tips for organizing your life. There's even an article suggesting that maybe too much organization is not a good thing. Mostly though, it's about children. How to deal with your attention deficit child and the child's teacher, who might be skeptical.

In the writing class I teach, a woman recently turned in an

---

1. Michelle P. Kraus, *Allen Ginsberg: An Annotated Bibliography, 1969–1977* (Scarecrow Press, 1980), 66.

essay about her son who suffers from attention deficit. Her essay was written as a love letter and was completely absent of hate or envy or any of the things that make us human. It was missing everything we try to hide.

"How are you feeling?" my psychiatrist asks.

"Better," I reply.

I had stopped taking the pills for a year, maybe more. Three weeks ago I started taking them again. When I quit taking Adderall I was still dating Lissette. I would go to her house in Berkeley during the day while her husband was gone and wrap myself around her feet while she worked. Or I would visit her at the dungeon where she worked on the weekends as a professional dominatrix. I would sit in the dressing room with the women and we would watch television. Lissette was the most popular and she would be off with clients most of the day. She would leave them in the rooms to undress. When she returned they would be kneeling on the floor, their naked backs facing her. She might walk carefully toward them, sliding the toe of her boot across the carpet. Or she might stand away from them, letting their anticipation build, as she pulled a single-tail from the rack. She loved to be adored and the best clients made her feel happy and complete. The walls were thin and I could hear the paddles landing on a client's back with a thud sometimes followed by a scream. When she was done she might come downstairs and sit on my lap for a while, and then we would go.

I have a memory of Lissette in the dungeon, which was really just a four-bedroom basic Californian with a driveway and a yard in a quiet town north of Berkeley, near the highway. She's standing on the back of a couch, grabbing a toy from the top of a row of lockers. She's wearing panties with lace along the bottom and high heels, and we're all staring at the back of her thighs, amazed.

When I was taking Adderall all I thought about was Lissette and when I stopped taking the Adderall I started thinking about other things. Lissette noticed and we broke up. Then we got back together, then we broke up again. Over the course of last year, after I had stopped, I often felt suicidal. I had time, but I didn't know what to do with it. I was a writer but I had forgotten how to write so I sat with my computer. I sat in coffeeshops or I sat at home or I sat at the Writer's Grotto, an old building near the ballpark where a group of authors share office space. I still had a bunch of pills left and occasionally I would take one, just to know that the writer's block was real. Then I lost all the pills when my bag was stolen at a bar on Twenty-second Street six months ago, and that was the end of that.

If you asked me what happened this past year I'm not sure I could tell you. I could say I moved into this apartment on the edge of the city where I can hear children and dogs in the morning and I despise it. I could say I was with and not with Lissette, getting together and breaking up every couple of months. At one point I called her the love of my life. I could say honestly I started to write a novel every day. I could say I went on tour for six weeks with the Sex Workers Art Show and that a compilation of previously written essays and stories about my predilection for—my addiction to—violent sex was released to silent reviews.

I could say I watched the first three seasons of *The Wire* on DVD and on Sunday nights I went to a friend's house nearby and ate dinner and watched HBO.

I ran a reading series in the same bar where my bag was stolen. The series was part of a literary organization I founded to raise money for progressive candidates running for Congress in 2006.

I edited an anthology of political erotica.

I could say I did all these things and if it sounds like a lot I can assure you it isn't. I'm not married and I have no children. I have friends but they don't know where I am most of the time. I don't work. I live on money I made before, money that is almost gone.

Last year I made $10,000.

I live in San Francisco. Rents are going up.

I'm teaching a couple of classes to get by. I know I should get a job, but it's hard to do that after a while.

On May 5, 2007, Floyd Mayweather meets Oscar De La Hoya at the MGM Grand Arena in Las Vegas. The fight has been hyped for five months. Floyd will make more than $20 million and De La Hoya will make more than $30 million. De La Hoya is heavier and Mayweather faster. Mayweather goes running late at night in Las Vegas, 3:00 AM sprints in the dark. The underlying drama is that Floyd's father had been in jail for drug running. Floyd trained with his uncle instead.

The boxers move quickly inside the ropes, sweat pouring down their backs like a glaze. Mayweather peppers the older De La Hoya, landing a shot in the tenth that snaps De La Hoya's head back like a spring toy. De La Hoya, well past his prime, comes out hard in the final rounds, his shoulders turning as if on rotors, delivering a flurry of jabs into Mayweather's ribs. Mayweather just barely wins the fight and tells anyone who will listen, "This proves I'm the greatest fighter of all time." But it doesn't. Floyd Mayweather was supposed to win big, and he squeaked by. Floyd's father sits ringside, a guest of his son's opponent. The father has long braids and cheeks so sharp it's as if his face was engraved. After the fight the older Mayweather says he thinks De La Hoya should have won.

I know everything there is to know about fathers who root against their sons.

The morning after the fight I get a call from Josh, a staff writer at *Wired* magazine. He's working on a profile of Hans Reiser, a brilliant computer programmer accused of killing his estranged wife.

I helped Josh track down Hans' former best friend, Sean Sturgeon. Sean and I have several girlfriends in common and I once did a bondage photo shoot in his apartment when he wasn't home. I don't remember ever meeting him but our paths have

crossed so many times it almost doesn't make sense. Josh is calling to say he found out something incredible about the case.
"Your guy Sean just confessed to eight murders, maybe nine."

"Why maybe nine?"

"He isn't sure if one of the victims was dead."

Josh says Sean's not under arrest and he's refusing to tell the
district attorney the names of the people he killed. Sean told Josh
that he confessed to the DA because he's a born-again Christian
and thought the jury would want to know. It seemed the right
thing to do. Or rather, he posed it as a question: "Don't you think
the jury would want to know?" But then he said Hans knew about
his murders and he was confessing in order to beat Hans to the
punch. Maybe he confessed for both reasons. Or maybe he confessed for reasons that had nothing to do with Reiser or the jury.
He denied having anything to do with Hans' wife's disappearance. He told Josh, "Give me some sodium pentothal or any truth
serum, put a little ecstasy in there and ask me if I killed Nina. I
have never been a threat to her."[2]

Sean told the police and the district attorney that his victims
had physically and sexually abused him and his sister in the East
Bay commune where they were raised. He claimed he hadn't
killed anyone since 1996. The commune interests me. I know the
places where adults come in contact with unsupervised children.
Between fourteen and eighteen I was in five different state-funded
childcare facilities, including three group homes, a mental hospital, and a temporary youth shelter that stuffed thirty children
into each room. In those places you can never tell who to trust.

When I'm done talking to Josh I feel like I'm waiting for something. The group homes were a long time ago. It's still morning
and I put a pot of water on the stove. I call Josh back and ask him
for Sean's phone number.

---

2. Josh Davis, *Wired*, June 26, 2007.

If Sean committed eight murders it's a huge story, I think. Here is a man willing to wait years to get revenge on the people who stole his childhood. I think of *In Cold Blood* and *The Executioner's Song*, two of my favorite books, both set around spectacular murders and written by novelists. I know people who have known Sean for more than a decade. I have the inside track. And there's something else about the case; Nina Reiser's body was never found.

But I'm getting ahead of myself. I don't know if Sean will talk to me. If he did kill eight people, surely the police would have arrested him by now. And why isn't he a suspect in the disappearance of Nina Reiser?

After calling Sean and leaving a message I bicycle through the city, down Market Street toward the Castro, my right pant leg rolled up so as not to get caught in the chain. My bicycle, an old Peugot I picked up for $150 nine years ago, is my prize possession. I live a spare existence. I haven't owned a car since I first got to this city.

I cut right, past the Gay and Lesbian Center and the Three Dollar Bill Café. Something's tugging on me. I had heard of Nina's murder, but never the full story. I had heard about Sean and how Nina's disappearance crushed him. He took to bed, paralyzed with grief. He was in love with his best friend's wife. It was all just passing information. But eight murders? Revenge killings? Eight murders isn't revenge. Eight murders is a serial killer.

I go to the park to meet a girl I know. Someone who has taken a habit of coming to my readings. She's engaged and lives with her fiancé between the Marina and Russian Hill. I've only seen her once before and she'd explained their relationship. It was simple. He was monogamous and believed in monogamy. She cheated on him and always would.

She arrives wearing a black dress and sandals. Her skin is so pale all I can think of is milk. I don't think of my complicity in her unfaithfulness. I don't want to. I don't love her; she's just someone I know. I wait as she walks across the grass in her sandals. A man stops her and asks if she is willing to be in one of his paintings. She talks with him for a moment, her head turned his way, her body pointing toward me. He doesn't have any paint. He wears dark, heavy clothes, his belongings bound in garbage bags around him.

The sun is brilliant and the colorful houses are brightly lit along the hills. On some days the fog catches on their drainpipes like cotton, but today it's easy to see why people want to live here. Easy to see San Francisco for the gentle paradise it is.

We lie on the grass with my shirt pulled up. I forget all about De La Hoya's fight and Sean Sturgeon's confession. I ask her to pinch my nipple and she does but it isn't enough. I ask her to do it harder and soon there is blood everywhere. There are people nearby but they don't seem to notice. For most of it she keeps her hand over my mouth and I close my eyes and drift away. "It's OK," she says.

That's only half the day. There's a barbecue, and then a reading, and then a party. There's always a party. I dance with a girl. "How do you know Eric?" I ask between songs. "I don't," she says. "My boyfriend knows him." I dance better after that. It's still the weekend, after all. It's still San Francisco. Everything is beautiful. Really. It seems perfect. The DJ looks like Napoleon Dynamite and spins pop from the eighties on vinyl. I'm thirty-five years old. The woman I'm dancing with has curly black hair and moves with steady grace, her silk dress rolling in waves down her arms. I feel loose and fine. I take $5 from another writer, who puts his money, inexplicably, on De La Hoya.

"Always bet on youth," I tell him.

It's one in the morning. I don't imagine anything can ever go wrong.

I'm leaning back at my desk staring at a poster for Cameron Tuttle's Paisley Hanover when Sean finally returns my call. "You're a hard guy to get a hold of," I say.

"I needed to do a little research on you first," he replies. He sounds friendly and sure of himself. Like someone who knows he has something you want but hasn't decided if he'll give it to you.

I get right to the point and ask for the names of the eight people he killed.

"I'm not ready to talk about that yet," he says. "Let's just say there are fewer abusers on the street now than there were before."

He wants to know if I think he should get a literary agent.

I say I think he should get a lawyer.

"Why do I need a lawyer?" he asks. "I'm ready to plead guilty and spend my time in prison as a good Christian."

"They're not going to put you in jail without knowing who you killed."

"Why do they have to know *who* I killed? Isn't the confession enough?"

I tell him he doesn't need a literary agent.

I'm talking with a man who has already told the police he killed eight people. I imagine they're investigating, or they don't believe him.

"I've been asking around," Sean says. "People have a lot to say about you." I let that lie between us. Something about the way he says it makes me not want to know. And I don't want to admit too many acquaintances in common. I don't want to put anybody in danger, or at least anybody other than myself.

It turns out he's been speaking with Lissette. They know each other from the dungeon. He used to be the houseboy and when one of the girls wanted to practice with her whips she would practice on him. "I hear you're emotionally dishonest," Sean says. That's what Lissette told him. It's exactly the kind of accusation she would make. Her accusations are like koans. I think, *You killed eight people and you're accusing me of being emotionally dishonest?*

After talking for a few minutes Sean and I make plans to meet in Oakland then hang up. It's the first I've heard of Lissette since our latest breakup. She knew about Sean's confessions, but she was talking with him anyway, even as she was packing her apartment outside the financial district and moving to the fog belt on the edge of Golden Gate Park. She had left her husband and then she had left me. Of course, it's more complicated than that. Every relationship is. She would never have left if I fought harder to keep her. She was a jealous girlfriend, and when she told me all the ways I made her unhappy, I never really understood. I probably wasn't trying hard enough. Or I wasn't capable.

Lissette used to cut me. She kept a knife by my bed, a present from a client. It had a grip handle. My breathing would slow down when the blade opened my skin. I would close my eyes and feel my body lift from the mattress. It was like being on a raft. One time I was blindfolded and my chest was bleeding and

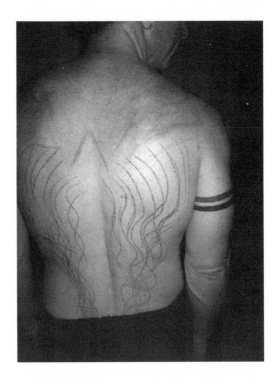

I tried to kiss her while pushing up against the knife, which she held to my jugular.

"You have no sense of self-preservation," she said, planting kisses on my cheeks.

It wasn't true. I had a fantastic sense of self-preservation but it had left me for a while.

She woke me one night two months ago in her large studio in the busiest part of San Francisco and said she thought I should leave. I said I was sorry I couldn't make it work. I had been sleeping naked on the inside of the spoon. She was so beautiful and she looked at me the way a mother looks at a child and I loved that. I put my clothes on and bicycled home across the city. The landscape of closing bars and well-lit taquerias seemed bright, surreal, and full of smoke.

I didn't tell Sean about that.

I didn't tell Sean I found a book of mine in the used bookstore near my house. I don't know how they got it. I self-published it years ago and then took it out of print. It was like finding an old diary. It was full of stories written in my early twenties, most of them centering on my relationship with my fiancée, Josie. The plot was: a good girl from a good family falls in love with an artist and betrays him by treating him the same way he treats her. I recognized the boy in the stories, many of them written from the girl's perspective. I thought he was very normal for his age, a little lost. He was a boy who saw the world through narrative; people and events all had arcs. Life tapered toward a conclusion. I can see now that there is a conclusion but no arc. There's life and death and all the barely connected things that happen in between. The boy I read about was a boy who could have settled on something and turned out OK. What he needed was a goal. Instead he went traveling because he thought he was happier when he was alone.

Yesterday there was a tornado in Kansas. People are angry because the equipment they need is in the Middle East. I see the news in a crowded bar where I'm watching the second round of the play-offs. Utah has called a time-out and for a minute the station rolls pictures of splintered houses and turned-over cars. The governor wants to call out the National Guard but the Guardsmen are serving tours overseas. Then a solemn reporter grips the microphone. The sound is turned off so I can't hear what he's saying, just read the capsule summaries below the screen.

There's a table set up with free hot dogs. A boy in his early twenties drinks near the window. His girlfriend comes in just before the half and kisses him on the cheek. She presses her side against him. It makes me think of Josie, the way she would sit next to me.

It was the summer of 1995 when we first got together. She had just graduated college, was drinking heavily and preparing to travel in Europe. While she was away I sent long letters, up to forty pages, *poste restant* to whichever town she was heading to next. They weren't love letters so much as diaries written by hand.

Two years later we were living in Chicago's Ukrainian Village. By then I'd overdosed on heroin and Josie was overcoming a cocaine habit. We spent time on our front porch. The neighborhood was changing. Rents were going up, but it wasn't there yet. It was a long way from there. There was so much concrete and if you looked east, the concrete rose from the ground and became the buildings downtown. We weren't far from Harpo Studios, where Oprah ran her empire. We were miles from the lake and the city was hot and the Village was all red brick and white cement. I don't remember there being any parks in that neighborhood. Josie had a job at a recruiting firm downtown but I couldn't seem to do it. I worked temp assignments but was always getting fired.

"Why don't you get me a job?" I asked.

"I will," she promised.

Josie had convinced me to return to Chicago with her. I had been living in Los Angeles for six months working as an assistant on a TV show called *Second Noah,* about adolescents whose parents had died, or whose parents had abandoned them, and who'd been taken in by a family in Florida. It was supposed to be a modern version of *The Brady Bunch* but the producers had no understanding of what happens to children of that age without parents. When the show was canceled I got work as a driver and stole all of the presents out of Leonardo DiCaprio's fan mail, which I was delivering from his agent to his publicist, and gave them as Christmas presents. One of the presents was sheer silk underwear, which I gave to Josie. But they were cut for men and drooped sadly around her thighs. On the drive back from LA, Josie and I almost got married at a twenty-four-hour chapel in Las Vegas, but didn't. To make up for it I bought her an engagement ring from a quarter machine at a K-Mart outside Salt Lake City and we slept the night in the parking lot during a snowstorm. We were twenty-four.

The apartment we ended up with in Chicago was long, with high ceilings. The landlord left threatening, incoherent notes. There was a man on the corner who sold elotes on a stick covered in butter and cheese. We were just two miles, maybe less, north of the United Center where Michael Jordan played.

What I'm trying to say is that I loved Josie, but things didn't work out.

A year later Josie went off to law school in Washington, D.C. She offered to stay in Chicago with me and attend a lesser school but I said I didn't want to be responsible for her bad decisions. Then I was accepted at the University of Virginia Law School; I'd taken the Law School Admission Test at Josie's urging and scored well. I could start the next year and Josie and I would be within easy driving distance. We could hike the Blue Ridge Mountains. I broke up with her instead.

"I just thought we would always be together," she said. And I know part of me felt good about it, like I had won.

For two years, more, before we stopped talking altogether, Josie wouldn't take me back. She met someone else, fairly quickly. Because she was desirable. And I mean not just beautiful, but the kind of woman who smiles a lot, and likes to have a good time, and thinks for herself. She had confidence. She was fun to be around.

Five years after Josie and I split I met her on a train. It was a coincidence. There were ten cars, so even on the same train the odds were stacked against us. I was spending a weekend in a city I didn't live in anymore and I thought she had moved away. But there she was in a polyester sleeveless brown shirt, without makeup, reading a paperback. She was like everybody else on that train, coming home from work, except she had better posture. I sat next to her, reading over her shoulder, and she ignored me until I started to poke her. Then she turned and we started to laugh.

"What in the world," she said, shaking her head and smiling, closing the book on her lap.

She looked lovely, but not as lovely as she would have looked if she had known she was going to see me. If she'd had her lipstick on and some blush, I don't know what I would have done. As it was, she was working as a lawyer for the labor relations board and getting married to Tony, who was one of my best friends from college. We were no longer on speaking terms.

I convinced her to get a drink with me and we went to a bar where the pipes were broken and water poured from the ceiling into buckets set across the floor.

"This is wonderful," I joked. "We're having a drink inside our metaphor."

Eventually Tony came and by that time I was very drunk. He was still tall, muscular, and strikingly handsome. I considered hitting him but that was unlikely to turn out in my favor.

"Why didn't you tell me you were dating her?" I asked Tony. "I'd have gotten over it eventually."

"It was you or Jo, and I picked Jo," he said.

After a little more talk Tony said they were considering a move to North Carolina.

"Why would you do that?" I asked.

"Property's cheap," Tony said. "And there's less crime."

They lived in a condominium Tony's parents owned in a run-down building at the end of Lake Shore Drive. The neighborhood hadn't changed in years. There was no more crime now than before, but they were talking about something else.

Earlier today I talked with a woman I know in Virginia. I locked the door to my office, turned on the camera in the computer, and took my clothes off for her. She told me to turn around and I did. Then I sat naked at the computer and typed. It was ridiculous. I also spent the day preparing for class. If I can keep teaching I'll be fine. Not really, but I'll have enough money to make it for a little while. The classes are ending in a couple of weeks and I have nothing new scheduled. If I agree to move to some small town that needs a professor I can get on the tenure path. I could buy a house and teach people how to write. I'd have to sleep with my students then. Away from the big city it would be my only option. But that's not really open to me. It's not really what I want to do. Which is what got me on this track to begin with, arranging interviews with murderers, hoping to make sense of somebody else's crime. There's a woman missing. Her husband says he didn't kill her. There's a man who says he's killed eight people but won't say who they are. There are so many unanswered questions. It's been a long time since I knew what I wanted, since I had something to strive toward. I keep floating, head poking above the waves, waiting for a purpose to arrive like a boat in the middle of the ocean.

I never did meet anyone like Josie again. Women like Josie don't make it to their thirties without getting married. If you're going to meet someone like that you're going to meet her in your early twenties. And if you're like me, that's going to be a time when you're making your living selling drugs out of your freezer, living in a squat a bullet away from Cabrini Green. You'll have to represent something, like the other side of the tracks, but safe. Someone who, when the time comes, when the party's over, she can turn around and guide to a place where life is a little more predictable. But when the party was over I didn't want to turn around. I didn't want to go to law school or get a real job or love only one person forever though in many ways she was the most loveable person I was ever going to meet. It didn't matter. I had to test my dissatisfaction. She had gone east so I went west. I got a job in a ski resort, bartending on top of a mountain. I learned how to board, and disappeared in the snow.

That was another time. I've been in San Francisco nine years. I'm suffering side effects from the Adderall. There are always side effects. Insomnia, loss of appetite, headaches, obsession, erratic decision-making. Inconsistency. I took my pill early in the day but I'm still awake and full of thoughts. So I lie in bed with my windows open, glad to be alone. It's the middle of the week. I haven't been sleeping and I'm missing appointments. My nails are bitten down and bleeding. All I can do is document it all and see where it leads me. I'm taking my meds and the world will be a different place for a while.

I have a self-published book I wrote when I was with Josie, and another book of unpublished poems. I never show them to anyone. The poems are so full of anger. Anger at Josie for being better than me, for always having the upper hand. For loving her family and being loved by them in return. For being someone who got over things and not recognizing that I was a person who didn't get over anything. But I read that book and those poems and I see something else. I see who I was then.

This is who I am now.

CHAPTER 2

Late May; Tom Takes the Ball; Once Upon a Time in
the Mental Hospital; Hans Reiser at Alameda County
Courthouse; Sean Sturgeon in Oakland; In Bed with
Miranda

On a warm Sunday afternoon I meet some friends at a court above the Castro. We run three on three, protected from the wind by Buena Vista Hill. We play a soft game. No one wants to be injured. From the court we can see the next hill rising before Noe Valley and east to the long flat space of the Mission District before Portero Hill and the piers.

"I can score on you at will," Doug says, which is mostly true. I'm not a good player. For some reason I've always been drawn to basketball, even though I was more talented at other sports. Doug grabs my shirt and I threaten to start a blog about him, dougcheats.blogspot.com. My team wins every game.

After, Tom asks if I would like a ride to my bicycle, which is down at the intersection. I say sure, just to put off being alone. I tell him about an email I came across while searching for an old girlfriend's phone number. In the email she said she was angry. She said I only called her when my "needs" were acting up. That I didn't think of her as a person.

"We're all like that at times," Tom says. "You shouldn't worry about it. I think you're one of the most well-adjusted people I know. I mean, outside of your love life."

"Really?" I say. "You think that?"

"Sure," he says. "Considering the life you've led. Don't you think so?"

I shake my head and smile, then get up and walk him back to his car. I don't think so. I don't think so at all.

When I was fourteen I slept on a couch in my old house. It was the house I grew up in, a yellow stucco corner home with a magnolia tree in the backyard. The house was mostly empty. My father was selling it. He had already moved to a new place in the suburbs somewhere. I had been on the streets for almost a year, sleeping in hallways and on rooftops. On particularly cold nights I had broken into boiler rooms. I knew it was dangerous to sleep in my old house.

I dreamed of footsteps, then screams, then something hitting my face. I woke trying to hide from my father's fists. He pulled me by my hair into the kitchen where he had a set of clippers waiting. He forced me to kneel at the cabinets while he shaved my head. It was the second time he had shaved my head. There wasn't any reason for it, except perhaps control through humiliation. He didn't know what else to do. I had put a cigarette out on the windowsill.

He gave me $5 when he was done, then went to the local pharmacy and told them not to sell me any razors. It was early in the morning and we sat outside the pharmacy and he placed his hand on my shoulder and said something conciliatory.

"I hate you so much," I said.

When the police found me that night sleeping beneath the mailboxes in the entryway to an apartment building, I had a giant gash in my wrist. I had gone to a different pharmacy for razor blades. It was my sixth suicide attempt that year.

"Where do your parents live?" they asked.

"I don't know," I said. All I knew was the location of the empty house. That was the night I fell into the Illinois juvenile system. The officers stared at me lying there, the room lit by the flashing red and blue lights filtering through the windows, like in some twisted disco.

The hospital they took me to was on the northwest side surrounded by a field of weeds and crabgrass and a tall fence, a place for abandoned children called Henry Horner Children's Adolescent Center. It's been closed down for years but it was the kind of place you'd never end up in if you had someone advocating for you. There were no towels, no soap, no doors on the washroom stalls. The inmates punched the air and spread shit in long brown streaks across the walls.

and depression as well as develop a clearer perspective of his family.

3) Custody should remain with DCFS as both Steve and his father are locked in a destructive pattern. This was evident in this one situation: Steve desperately needed clothing, father agreed to pick up some of Steve's clothing that had been left at various friend's homes in the last few months. However, father would not bring them in unless Steve would accept the clothing from his hand. Steve verbally refused to accept clothing from his father. Thus, father did not pick them up and stated that if Steve would not do it his way, he would have nothing more to do with it. There are other incidences that are too lengthly to include in this report.

4) Steve's paternal uncle, Dr. Ronald Blum, has expressed an interest in having Steve live with him in Baltimore, Maryland. Exploration of this possibility should be sought.

Nancy Sidum, Psy.D.
Psychologist III
HHCC - B-East

October 16, 1986

NS:mw

The year on the streets had drained me. I'd followed a man into a hotel room and sat at a plastic table snorting lines of coke while a john with a black mustache and blond wig wearing a nurse's dress sucked off two or three homeless men at a time. I'd hitchhiked to California with my best friend and spent three days in the Las Vegas detention center. I slept with strangers, ate out of garbage bins, panhandled for change. I got in cars every time a driver opened a door. I'd become too adept at moving around. It was good for me to stay in one place for three months with locked exits and a bed.

The hospital was filthy but there was heat, televisions bolted near the ceiling in the day room, a pool table. The children were doped up on Thorazine and Haldol and walked around like zombies. The point of the pills was to keep the children manageable but I was so subdued when admitted they didn't bother. I made friends with Jay, who had burned down a church, and Malcolm, who had unsuccessfully tried to kill his stepfather. I hung out with French Fry, who was tall and good looking with thick black hair, but three fourths of his body was covered in mottled red scars from lighting himself on fire. We played cards throughout the day and smuggled in pot, which we hid inside the foam roof panels. At lunch we smacked butter patties onto the ceiling and they turned rancid so they stopped giving us butter. When Malcolm was placed in restraints I slid a magazine below the door so he would have something to read. I was reprimanded and locked in timeout, a small room with a thin mat and a window on the hallway for staff to look in.

When a bag of thirty ice-cream cups was discovered in one of the freezers the janitor asked who it belonged to. "That's Carol's," I said, referring to a nurse who had problems with her weight. I was put in timeout again.

One night, staff was lecturing us on our bad attitudes and one of them said, "You act like you're in hell." And French Fry stood screaming. "You want to see hell, motherfucker? I've seen hell!"

Shortly after my phone call with Sean Sturgeon I head to Alameda County Courthouse. I take a rush-hour train to Oakland surrounded by all the other morning people with places to be.

It's the beginning of Hans Reiser's trial and I've been gathering information on the case, unsure whether Hans will be at the periphery or center of my true crime book. Hans met Nina in 1998 when he visited a bridal office in St. Petersburg, Russia. His company was doing well and he had hired several Russian programmers to help with the next generation of the file system he'd been working on. He paged through the women's profiles, paying $20 for each one he wanted to be introduced to. The women would come in to a conference room for fifteen minutes and if he liked them they made other plans. Nina Sharanova didn't want to come to the office so her profile was marked "phone first." She was the last woman Hans contacted and they arranged to meet near the Church of the Spilled Blood where Alexander II had been slain in 1880, one link in a chain of events leading to the October Revolution of 1917.

Hans met more than fifty women through the service but Nina was different. She had a quality he couldn't fully understand, a sincerity of affection he'd never experienced with the exception of his mother. But she wasn't his mother and her affection wasn't only for him. She was magnetic, beautiful, easygoing. When she walked into a room people turned to look at her. It's easy to see, even in the photographs. The high, fine cheekbones, the easy smile. She never looks like she's posing for a picture. A woman like Nina had never paid attention to Hans before.

At their first meeting Hans read Nina a poem and told her he was a famous computer programmer. Maybe she thought he was like Bill Gates. As it happens, in the world of open source computer programmers and techno geeks, Hans Reiser is a minor celebrity. His file system, ReiserFS, was the first journaling file system for Linux. The journal is the computer's own imperfect story. It's like the black box in an airplane cockpit, but it's also the flight plan, a record of what the computer did as well as where it intended to go. Storing data on a disk, like committing an event to memory, is almost never a one-step process. If the computer gets interrupted between steps, the file system becomes inconsistent, the computer crashes, and certain data is lost forever. The journal allows a computer to recover from this catastrophe by resolving inconsistencies, reconciling what can be known with what can't, providing the narrative bridge between where the computer has been and what the machine has become. If ReiserFS became a standard feature of the open source operating system Linux, distributors would pay Hans' company for support and Hans would be worth millions. The only stumbling block was Hans' personality. In a community known for eccentric personalities, he had a reputation for being selfish and aggressive and particularly difficult to work with.[3]

A year after they met, Nina was in America, pregnant with their first child. Hans was frequently away in Russia supervising his team of programmers, and Sean was hanging around keeping Nina company. According to Sean he warned Hans he needed to be more involved in his marriage and sent Hans two books, *The Dummies Guide to Better Communication Between Couples* and *The Dummies Guide to Divorce*. He told Hans he was going to need one of those books.[4]

In 2001 Sean and Nina had their first affair. In California Nina helped Hans with his company, but Hans' father told him she

---

3. It is not universally agreed upon that the ReiserFS is the first Linux journaling system but the majority of programmers believe it to be the first. A majority also agree that the reason ReiserFS never made it to the Linux kernel was because of Hans' difficult personality. There are also programmers that claim Hans stole the basic code for the file system.
4. Nearly two years after first speaking with Sean I find out Books In Print does not list these titles, although it does list *Divorce for Dummies*.

was embezzling money. She was a doctor and wanted to pass the American medical boards but Hans wanted her to stay home and take care of the kids. He said he didn't have any use for a smart wife. He told her that in America it was just as respectable to be a good mother as it was to be a doctor. Nina wanted to be both. She filed for divorce in the summer of 2004, leaving Hans for his best friend. The divorce was contentious, with Hans adopting his father's claims and accusing Sean and Nina of embezzling money.

If I'm going to write a true crime book I'm going to have to figure out what happened between Hans and Nina and Sean. Like Hans, Sean had a motive for killing Nina; she left him as well. In 2005 Nina met Anthony Zografos, an attractive older man with a husky Mediterranean accent and large, sad eyes. She continued to accept money from Sean but refused to see him. Sean left $1,900 in cash in Nina's mailbox two days before she disappeared. According to Anthony, Nina thought Sean was a psychopath.

On September 3, 2006, Nina dropped the children with Hans for the weekend and was never seen or heard from again. Hans' father suggested she was probably hiding in Russia. Two weeks later the police found a copy of *Homicide* by David Simon in Hans' car.[5] Simon, who also created the TV show *The Wire,* says there are two types of murder cases, the dunkers and the whodunits. The dunkers are slam-dunks, involving, say, a man covered in blood standing over a body saying, "Yeah, I killed him. He hit me first." The dunkers are easy. The whodunits take time. You have to interview people, gather evidence. And even when you do everything right there's all that space between the arrest and the trial, so much opportunity, so easy for the killer to get away. Simon says a suspect should never talk to the police. He also says

---

5. The car actually belonged to his mother, but she rarely drove it.

that a murder is rarely solved without a body. Without a body you have to first prove the person is dead.

When I arrive at the court I meet Henry Lee from the *San Francisco Chronicle*. He's alone on a bench in the hallway trying to get reception for a tiny battery-powered transistor television. Henry's a veteran crime reporter and his byline accompanies many of the major cases in the Bay Area. I ask what he thinks of Sean's confession and how he thinks it will impact the case. He can't write about Sean's confession because of a gag order. Henry says the confession is "fantastical." He says, "People confess to murders they didn't commit all the time."

It's just preliminary hearings. A judge has to be assigned, a jury selected. The prosecution and the defense have to argue over what evidence will be admissible.

I watch the public attorneys in their wrinkled suits. They look just like the men and women I saw periodically in my youth introducing themselves as my guardian *ad litem*. Or filling out the forms admitting me into the mental hospital. Or picking me up from the group home I lived in deep on the South Side, driving me along Lake Shore Drive, past the giant steel mountains of downtown, and leaving me at the next group home on the North Side. They were there when my friend and protector was removed and placed in drug rehab. They were there for twice-yearly progress meetings on the West Side where I was left with an ashtray and a stack of magazines while they decided what would happen to me next. They were there when my father was found guilty of abuse and neglect, and all the other times. They always looked like they hadn't showered or shaved or brushed their hair. Their shirts were misbuttoned, often untucked. But they always had buttons on their shirts. They always had collars. And they drove small, messy cars.

These are the people in the court, along with the bailiffs, the judge with a face like a teddy bear, the prisoners off to one side of the room, another box for medium and maximum security prisoners, and the friends and families sitting in various shades of sweat-suit cotton on the dark wood seats. It's crowded but orderly. People know each other. There's a lot of smiling and nodding and shuffling of papers, while decisions are handed down, permanently altering people's lives. When I was young, my father warned me about getting caught in the gears of the system. The system, he said, would not let go once you were inside. The machine would grind you to dust.

But it happened anyway and I'm still alive.

In pre-trial motions Hans waives his right to a speedy trial. His lawyer has another murder to litigate. There's no date for seating a jury. I think about this trial, and where it's going to go. Will it grind Hans to dust or will he emerge to complete his next file system? A computer can't run without a file system. It wouldn't be able to find anything. The hard drive would be like a library with a billion unshelved books and no card catalog. The county clerk, tapping a polished nail on the partition, her untucked shirt hanging loosely over her skirt, leans over to talk with the court reporter. And it occurs to me that at some point in my life I should have been one of them, a probation officer or a caseworker, if just for a while. It was the logical thing for a group home kid to do.

There's a small line of cabs waiting at the MacArthur Bart Station. The drivers sit on their hoods or lean back in their seats reading newspapers. A pushcart vendor sells Cokes and pretzels, high school students wait around the bus stop. Oakland lacks all of the charm of San Francisco. The breeze is warmer, the colors are dull, the roads are flat and poorly maintained, the school system is a wreck. It's a muscular city, dangerous in parts, a different kind of California.

I look around for Sean but don't see him. In a note he sent following our phone call he claimed we had met before at the Berkeley pier but I have no memory of that. I remember a birthday party and a barbecue and a fight I had with Lissette. But I don't remember Sean.

I've seen pictures of Sean but they weren't distinctive. They weren't the kind of pictures that give you a real sense of what the person looks like. And then I see a man standing by the rail at the car park and I see why he wouldn't stand out. He's pale and a little short, slightly fat, wearing jeans and a loose black top. He's unshaven and tired looking. On his neck is a faded blue ink cross, his face is lightly pocked, his red hair is going gray. He keeps his hands in his jeans and slouches forward. Like the city he lives in, he's drained of color, except for his eyes, which are a deep blue like a protected lake.

"I used to be quite handsome," he says. "Now I can't stay awake for more than a few hours." He says he's had surgery on his shoulder, another operation for kidney stones. Workers' comp kept him waiting a long time. He's been strung out on Vicodin for years.

We talk about Nina. "I took care of her," Sean says. "Even when she wouldn't see me."

I ask him questions and he won't give me the specifics. Or he will, but not the ones I want. He was born into the middle of an American story. It was the sixties, then the seventies. The Summer of Love had devolved into violent protests and a country split by an unnecessary war an ocean away. Flower children and peaceniks gave way to Charlie Manson, Altamont, bank robberies, guards shot dead at point-blank range, Richard Nixon, and bombs. It was a generation that failed to stop a war and, in Sean's case, failed to protect its children. He says he was molested and tortured over a period of thirteen years.

He lived in a commune near Berkeley, the epicenter of the movement. There were lots of communes then, filled with people protesting the war in Vietnam. Men were coming home from that war and dropping out. And some of those men were getting involved in the anti-war movement, and some of those men had bad memories from the Mekong Delta. And some of those men moved into Sean's house.

"So, are you writing about children who have been abused?" Sean asks.

"No," I say. "I'm writing about a person who's taken justice into his own hands and killed eight people."

"Why would I talk to you about that?" he asks.

We walk past an auto shop and a Walgreen's. The weather has gotten cold again. The sidewalks are battered and cracked. He tells me about these men, the men who came into the commune. Some, he says, had been trained at the School of the Americas. "Do you know about that place?"

"I do," I say. The academy, set up by the U.S. government to train South American soldiers, has been associated with the death squads in El Salvador and Chile and the Nicaraguan Contras. It was one of those sad American mistakes, a bad idea gone worse. But America does good, too. The CIA is involved in everything. We're not always on the wrong side. Usually we're on both sides, which means we're probably right at least 50 percent of the time. He talks about torture, what we see on the news, foreign soldiers detained, humiliated, drowned. Hundreds of pictures we've grown used to seeing. A man standing on a crate holding two electrical wires, unsure if he's about to be electrocuted. "That's nothing," Sean says. "That's not torture."

Sean says he's not into BDSM anymore and that he never did BDSM with Nina. He used to be what people refer to as a "heavy player," which is how we know so many people in common. I've heard of him digging a knife in his own arm, carving RAGE, or standing naked in the middle of a room while several women strike at him with leather straps, his blood pooling at his feet. But that was before he became a Christian. Now he goes to church every week, volunteers at the soup kitchen on weekends.

"Why should I talk to you?" he asks. "If someone was shooting at me right now, they might hit you. I don't want any more violence." I try to understand what he's saying. Who are these people who would shoot at us if he talked to me, and how would they find us? I imagine diving for cover as a car streaks past, faces hidden behind scarves, guns poking from the windows, the vehicle exhaling a gusher of exhaust thick as a mudslide. He thinks people might come after him, friends perhaps of the people he killed. It's as if the only reason he hasn't named his victims is to protect people like me and other innocent pedestrians. It's a bizarre rationalization, and the challenge is to figure out if he's afraid of going to jail or if he is lying. And why. He says he's never killed anyone who didn't abuse him. Then he adds, "Or came after me with a gun. You have to break some eggs to make an omelet." I try to get him to go further with this. What omelet? But he won't say anything more about it.

Sean says he never sought attention. This is clearly important to him, a matter of honor. He is ready to go to jail but unwilling to name the people he killed. He isn't sure why he should talk to me and I'm not sure either and I know this could go on for a long time.

But I'm stuck. I want information. An author looking for a story can be like a junky looking for a fix. But it's worse than that because an author without a story isn't even an author. I was ten or eleven when I started writing poems, which I brought to my friend's house to read to his mother. By the time I was twelve my bedroom was covered with poetry I'd taped to the walls. When my father ripped the poetry down, I kept writing, but hid it somewhere else. It was as if I had to express every thought that came into my head. The poems became longer, turning into stories during college. At some point my nervous brain stopped pumping out information so quickly, and I started publishing what I wrote. My reasons for writing changed. I was no longer trying to express every thought, I was writing to understand myself. I re-wrote my stories hundreds of times and became dependent on working through problems on the page. In my late twenties I was simultaneously awarded a fellowship for emerging writers and sold two novels I had submitted blindly to a small publisher. At that point I finally thought of myself as a writer. Other writers often called me prolific, which made me vaguely uncomfortable. It sounded more like an accusation than a compliment. Without paying attention I had become what I wrote and I worried what would happen if I became unable to write. And then one day it happened. And it happened the next day, and the day after that. And it lasted for almost two years with the exception of a vignette here or there. I'd gone silent. But now here was Sean.

We walk for an hour. Sean's friendly. I'm trying to decide if I like him, and I think I do. He mentions a man who was seeing an old girlfriend and how the man was giving him a hard time so Sean started surveiling him, keeping track of his habits, his whereabouts. This was only a few years ago. "I wouldn't have hurt him," Sean says. "I gave my guns to my pastor." He says he just wanted to convince this man to leave him alone, but the way he says it suggests something larger. Like the real message he was trying to get across to this man, and maybe to me, was that there were forces larger than himself at work in this world. By engaging Sean this man was coming in contact with things bigger than he could comprehend.

We talk about finding God.

"I've also been looking for something to give my life meaning," I say.

Sean tells me about the commune but doesn't give me names. He uses the word "hunting" to describe the periods he took off from work before 1996. He tells me about Julian Adams, a scoutmaster he claims was involved in a child molestation ring. "Look it up," he says. Later I do. Julian Adams had been convicted of lewd and lascivious behavior and a lawsuit against the Boy Scouts of America is still pending. He died of natural causes in 2004.[6] In our conversation Sean seemed to be hinting that he had something to do with Adams' death, but that's clearly false.

"So this is all off the record?" Sean says after a while.

We stop on a corner, facing each other.

"No," I say slowly. "I don't think so."

"Then let's go back," he says, turning toward the station.

I get a call and then a note from Sean. He writes, "I can see you're a person attracted to the limelight." He wants to sign a contract, something I had originally proposed. We should do a book together. Sean urges me to think big. He's considering a prison ministry and thinks his story of finding Jesus could help free the souls of people like him behind bars. But he's not yet in prison himself.

In the morning I take my pill and sit down at my desk. I think of taking an extra one just to go further, but I don't. I keep thinking about Sean and Hans. I keep getting Sean and Hans confused, perhaps because their names sound the same, or perhaps something else. I think about a young Sean, his pale arms poking from the blue sleeves of his dark blue scout uniform. I think about Nina Reiser and the two children she left behind, Cori and Lila, only four and six years old when their mother disappeared.[7] They're living with their grandmother in Russia now and it's unclear if she'll bring them back for the trial.

---

6. Alameda County Court File 98866.

7. Though widely printed elsewhere I've decided to use fake names for the children.

Sean said wolves mate once for life. He said he was Nina's wolf. When he pulled out of the Bart parking lot I saw a sticker of two wolves facing each other on his rear window. When I see my psychiatrist again I might ask her for sleeping pills. Something to help me so I don't stay awake all night thinking about murderers, and where they hide their thoughts. Something to help me hide my own.

I'm in bed with Miranda, a recent Stanford graduate. She's a friend of some of my former students and I feel a little strange about that. She just turned twenty-four. She's a burlesque dancer and a political activist. When she does her burlesque show she dresses like a maid and mops the floor with her hair and when she's done she's almost naked, shaking her shoulders with a sign taped across her chest: EXHIBITIONIST. In bed she wears boxer shorts and a tank top. She's tall and dark with kinky hair dyed with streaks of gold, a pierced lip, ivy tattoos circling above her hips. She could easily be a model, but she doesn't care. She believes in revolution.

Miranda grew up in Haiti, in a large house on a hill outside Port-au-Prince. All she'll tell me about her family is that her father works for a fruit company and doesn't agree with her views.

"What about your mom?" I ask.

She opens her mouth like she's going to say something awful, her tongue plastered against her bottom teeth, then shakes her head and pats me on the cheek. "You'd like my mother," she says. "You have a lot in common."

I hang out with Miranda in bars on Polk Street, watching her perform with drag queens. I meet a boy at her show, younger than me with a mohawk and a pretty face. He says he's also a writer, a poet. On the side he does boy burlesque. I think he's pretty, but if I were into men I would want someone stronger who could take care of me.

It's Patti Smith night and the queens climb the stage in black wigs and torn jeans. They sing "Ain't It Strange" and "Gloria," snarling at the crowd and wondering whose sins Jesus died for. Miranda dances behind them in a short skirt, kicking her long brown legs high in the air while I watch from the crowd, holding her drink.

Miranda's room is bright yellow with album covers stuck to the wall. Lene Lovich, Kate Bush, The Slits. She lectures me on music. I tell her she's a snob. We sleep on a small mattress. She insists I sleep naked and I insist she keep her clothes on. She wraps around my back, her arm over my chest.

Her windows face the morning sun and the illegals stand on the corner just below the ledge waiting for someone with a van and a job to stop and put them to work. They stand there every day, in baseball caps, sweatshirts. Waiting. Miranda says they aren't Mexicans; most of them are from Guatemala and El Salvador. I've been showing up at her place more and more often. I call from Valencia Street at the end of the day, just when I think she's going to sleep.

Hans' trial won't start for two more months. I was in court when they scheduled the hearing. It was my second time at the sturdy building in downtown Oakland. Hans wore yellow prison fatigues and stood in the prisoner's pen, holding two boxes of papers. I noticed his poor posture and thinning hair. He seemed naive, carrying the giant boxes and not understanding that the trial was actually months away.

"Tell me something nice," I said to Miranda the night after the hearing. I was acting like a child and she wanted desperately to be an adult. "Tell me I'm pretty."

"You are," she whispered. "You're so pretty."

Our relationship is absurd, infantilizing. I'm eleven years older than her. She's a vegan. She wears heels and keeps her sex toys on top of a beat-up dresser. She wants to dress me in women's clothes and I tell her I don't mind but I don't really think we'll get there.

The sad thing is how our relationship mirrors all my other romances. Fragmented. Thin. Except that I'm getting worse. In my twenties I would have been too proud to beg a woman to hold me. I didn't know enough to cry. I wouldn't dream of pressing my nose against someone's chest, saying, "I'm so sad. I don't know what's happening to me." And I have less to give.

We don't have sex. She has a girlfriend. And a boyfriend. She has many lovers. She keeps pictures of them on her desk, tapes their poems near the bed. She's so beautiful and smooth, like a statue cut from cherry. But for some reason I don't want to see her naked. Maybe she's too young, or something else. I'm just lying in bed with her, trying to fit into her stomach and not making it. She gets up to go to work at four in the morning, pulling on her boots while the city is still pitch. I rise with the sound of trucks stopping. On the surface everything seems fine.

In a note Sean says, "You have an opportunity to be a better person than you have been in the past and people are watching to see if you make the right decisions this time." He no longer wants to sign a contract. He says he isn't threatening me, but he's surprised I don't recognize him from before. "Maybe that's because you just view people and situations according to how they might or might not best serve your current interest."

He says he's having health problems and that he was assaulted as a result of the article Josh wrote about him. Then he disconnects his phone and stops answering his mail. In his notes to me the week before he disappears he mentions something Hans said to him. "Society has rules. And if society will not punish those who break the rules then I will."

I've only just started writing again and I'm not sure I'll be able to find the story without Sean. The trial seems a long way off. I can't stand another year of writer's block, sitting at a desk, staring out the window, waiting for something resembling insight to arrive like a packet in the mail.

Chapter 3

June; Minor Breakdowns and a Flight to Los Angeles;
The Part about Justin; Dungeon in San Fernando;
Nick Flynn on Torture; Paris Hilton; A Phone Call from
My Oldest Friend; Everybody Has a Murder Story

On June 5 Paris Hilton turns herself in at the Century Regional
Detention Facility in Lynwood. Her incarceration is the biggest
story of the year, almost comparable to that day in 1994 when
O. J. Simpson walked into the condominium on South Bundy
Drive, knocked his wife unconscious, pressed his knee into her
back, lifted her head, and slit her throat. Paris eclipses every-
thing. On June 7 the Los Angeles County Sheriff reassigns her to
home confinement. The next day the judge sends her back to jail.
Everywhere I go I see pictures of Paris Hilton or hear her name.
People talk about her, even while saying they're tired of talking about her. They talk about her then say we should really be
talking about Iraq. But the war is off the front page, along with
Phil Spector's murder trial and Britney Spears' comeback tour.
There's only Paris Hilton, her aquiline features and uniquely yellow hair, her small eyes staring at the rest of us.

When Sean disappears I head to the airport and purchase
a one-way ticket to Los Angeles. The first time I came to Los
Angeles was June 1986. I was nearing the end of my homeless
year. I hitchhiked with my best friend, Justin. Justin was a year

older than I and he had been running away since he was twelve.
I was supposed to be starting high school soon and Justin should
have been going into his sophomore year. But we didn't think
about that. We thought about places to sleep, listening to music,
and getting high.

Everything about Justin was cool: his long black hair, cheap
bandanas, the way he carried his cigarettes in his sleeve or in his
back pocket when he didn't have sleeves. He had an easy sense of
style but he was also very handsome; he would have looked good
no matter what he wore. Girls were always inviting him into their
houses when their parents weren't around. When he lived at home,
his father beat him with a stick, and sometimes Justin would tap
on my window at night, his entire body covered in welts.

Our plan was to get to California and become beach bums,
but we never made it to the beach. We got a ride across Arizona
from a trucker. He had a wife back East and called her from the
booths set aside for long-distance haulers at stops along the way.
He hardly even looked at the road, smoothly shifting the giant
gears as we drove west. He said he picked us up, even though it
was against company policy, because we looked harmless.

"I've been all over the country many times," he said. "Been to
Detroit and all points south. But where I'm dropping you kids is
East LA. And there ain't a thing in the world like East LA."

We arrived with no money, our clothes torn and caked in mud.
It had taken less than a week but we hadn't left with much. There
were hundreds, maybe thousands of trucks in the stop near the
interchange on the edge of downtown. Men stood in open trailers on piles of carpets, the air wavy with gasoline and radio bus-
tle. They hoisted barbells next to their trucks and blew smoke
from the windows. Nearby we found skid row where the homeless slept against the buildings or lined up for the soup kitchen.
There was vomit all over the sidewalks. The women looked as

THE ADDERALL DIARIES   51

though they would snap if you touched them. The buildings were boarded and abandoned or had sheets of metal pulled down their fronts. It was like a glimpse of our future. The homeless we knew in Chicago were like us, just kids with bad parents waiting for their situations to change. But near the Los Angeles Mission there were thousands of homeless people who were older and crazy and deathlike. They seemed to make up the entire city.

We left Los Angeles, hitchhiking north with a German tourist to Las Vegas where we were arrested. A couple days later I was sent back on a Trailways bus. The whole trip took eight days. Justin was let out of the juvenile hall two weeks after I was and when he got to Chicago he was taken into custody on an outstanding warrant for home invasion. His parents refused to pick him up and he was made a ward of the court. Two months later the state took custody of me as well.

Justin didn't tell me what had happened until eight years later, at a party in the apartment where I was living with new friends I had met in college. My college friends didn't like Justin; they thought he was a mooch. That night in Los Angeles eight years earlier, we had returned to the truck stop. A driver let us into his cab and we smoked hash with him. I remember how dark and shiny the driver's skin was, red and yellow sores weeping on his cheek. Or maybe my memory has altered his appearance so I see him with the swollen face of a demon. He made some calls over the radio, checking to see if any drivers wanted to take in a couple of young hikers. Of course, no one responded, and he had other plans. While I slept behind the seats he molested Justin and in the morning he stole our things, which was really just some poetry and a couple of shirts.

I was telling my favorite story, the one about hitchhiking to California with my best friend, and Justin interrupted me and said, "Steve, I was molested."

"Why didn't you say anything?" I asked. "Why didn't you scream?"

I meet a woman in Culver City. She's short and curvy with thick, bleached hair and lives in a complex at the intersection of two six-lane roads. The cars speed past like on a highway. I don't see how anybody could ever get across. Outside her apartment are lots filled with half-constructed buildings but nobody's working on them. Los Angeles is a place where things take a long time to happen.

It's eleven in the morning and before anything she wants to take her dog for a walk. There are no pedestrians on the bright white sidewalks and her dog takes a crap on the unfinished driveway in front of her neighbor's garage. She looks around, gripping a fistful of plastic bags.

"I'm not picking that up," she says.

I drive with her and her boyfriend through the hills of the 405, past the Getty, into the Valley. Everything is hot and flat, the grass is brown and weeds sprout from the walk. We stop in a 7-Eleven next to a gas station and load up on Red Vines and bottled water before turning into a nondescript alley and parking behind a low, windowless building with a thick iron door.

This used to be public storage. The entry is lit with low-wattage fluorescent bulbs. A woman sits at an old computer playing solitaire without acknowledging us. The house madam sits on a black couch near the entrance and we talk for a while before the four of us head into the second room where there's an eight-foot chain web against one wall, a leather bed, and a short, padded spanking bench with knee rests.

"This is a good place," the madam says. "As long as there aren't any customers. If a client comes he'll have to walk right through here to get to any of the other rooms."

"Are you ready?" she asks, running her fingers inside my shirt and pinching my nipples with her long nails.

"Yes," I say. It's too late to say anything else, and anyway, it feels good. I don't really want to know what's going to happen.

The house madam leaves and I take my clothes off and the woman from Culver City fastens leather cuffs around my ankles, latching a spreader bar to them to keep my legs forced apart. She fastens nipple clamps with weights on the ends, pushes me over the bed, and slides inside me with her strap-on. I'm wearing a rubber mask and a blindfold so I can't see her boyfriend moving behind us with the camera. She leans over me, one hand gripping my throat and the other pressing down my back. This is fine, I think. I'll just stay like this. When the filming is over and I'm getting dressed, the boyfriend offers me a can of energy cola. "You were great," he says. "We couldn't ask for a better victim."

It's not the first time I've been photographed nude, but it's the first video. When I was twenty-one and working as a stripper in Chicago, I was asked to make a porn. I made a demo, which consisted of masturbating while the director shot pictures with a small Kodak. But then I decided I didn't want to be in the film. I thought I might regret it. Now I know I wouldn't have regretted it. It wouldn't have meant anything.

At the time I was just out of college and didn't know what to do. In college I was a history major. I started hanging out at a club called Berlin, flirting with the bartenders and the cocktail servers. I had nowhere to go but I liked to dance. One night the bartender asked me to be in a fashion show. I walked the runway in striped shorts with orange straps across my shoulders, moving as slowly as I could, basking in the glow of the runner lights. A crowd of club-goers gathered along the sides and stretched their arms toward my ankles. I passed through the mesh curtains into the dressing room and asked if I could go again.

"You are so vain," the bartender said, patting my ass.

My stripper year was also my heroin year, when I headed with my friends to the West Side, through the remnants of the '68 riots, to pick up bundles from men on lawn chairs in front of abandoned lots.

At the same time I was just starting film school, and getting along better with my father. I would hang out at his house and we would tell each other stories, things that had nothing to do with my childhood. We never discussed what led to me leaving home so young and the state taking custody. We had different interpretations of what happened and if we got anywhere near the subject it felt like our fragile reconciliation wouldn't survive. My father would compliment me, tell me how much better my work was than the other film students. "They don't understand narrative," he said. "Most people don't know how to tell a story." He was proud of me, but not for working hard. Working hard was for suckers. He thought I had talents that other people didn't, talents that we shared. I soaked up his compliments but didn't trust him enough to share my feelings. I knew that if I admitted any vulnerability, someday he would use it against me. It was a feature of his rage. When he was angry he would grasp for whatever meant the most to you and destroy it. When I was with him I would tell him how well everything was going, how happy my life was, and when I left I replayed his compliments in my mind as if they were on a cassette and I was wearing invisible headphones.

One day I came over and my father was limping, his body twisting at right angles, his chest nearly parallel to the floor as he walked. Growling, he gripped the furniture, grasping the edges of the large white couches he'd bought with his new wife. "Motherfucker!" He turned to me, face red, eyes looking like they wanted to jump out of his skull. My big, strong, vain, and fearsome father with his beautiful body, always lifting weights so his chest and arms were thick, strutting naked through the house, past my mother and me, his cock flapping between his legs. But now he seemed broken. "My body is a burning building!" he shouted. "I have to get out!"

I felt a surge of emotion like I had never felt for my mother. My father left and I was alone in his big suburban house with the nice furniture. I cried for a long time, a deep, uncontrollable cry. Shortly after that his spine collapsed and he was placed in a halo and he moved to the first floor because he couldn't climb the stairs to the bedroom where he'd installed skylights. His new wife was trying to leave him and I said to her, "Now is the time." But she didn't, and I wasn't really that involved.

It was a period of my life that could have gone either way. Or maybe not. Maybe there's only one way to go with a needle. I went to school. I took my clothes off at The Manhole. Men ran their fingers along my legs, working their tips inside my underwear, trying to get a thumb in my asshole. I pressed my back against them at the Bijou Sunday mornings, rubbed my cheek against their necks. It all made sense at the time, twenty-two years old, a year out of college, graduate school, the rapprochement with my father, the nights and weekends spent dancing on a box bathing in anonymous attention, the rigs full of heroin. But when I try to make sense of it now it's like a soup. How could I be so many different people? My stripper year ended with an overdose in a rented room a couple of days before Thanksgiving, and when I got out of the hospital I spiraled into a period of unbearable depression. I was never the same after that.

Returning from the dungeon the woman's boyfriend drives my rental while I lay my head in her lap. She wears tight jeans and I press against her legs and she runs her fingers absently around my ear. A truck passes with a placard stuck to the sideboard: *We cheat the other guy and pass the savings on to you.* It takes a while in rush hour through the 405. She says she's hungry and wants to stop for Mexican food. I tell her I need to get back to Hollywood where I've been sleeping on my friend Bearman's couch.

I have no idea why I'm in LA. It's a city I've never liked. I'd been having the latest in a string of minor breakdowns. According to the book I'm reading these breakdowns are going to become more frequent, and more severe. But it doesn't happen. I start to feel better almost right away.

I sleep in the living room, near an open window, in an old-style courtyard building in a part of Hollywood known as Little Armenia. There's a fountain in the courtyard and a small hill where cats bathe in the sun. Beyond the gates old men set tables on the sidewalk and play backgammon until dusk. Bearman doesn't question why I'm in Los Angeles. He always seems genuinely happy to see me. He lives with his fiancée and people come over all the time. Everybody has keys. Nobody calls, they just walk in and out. There's no need to make plans. I take ten milligrams of Adderall with my coffee every day. At night, two milligrams of Lunesta gets me to sleep, but I wake up feeling groggy. The sleeping pills give me headaches. Or maybe it's the combination. I remind myself to eat, but sometimes I forget. In the mornings I meet Nick Flynn, who is writing a book about torture, and we sit across from each other with our headphones on. We met years ago after I reviewed a book he wrote. Now he's in LA with his girlfriend, who is starring in a new television series.

"It's not really about torture," he says. "It's really about me, and what it's like for me to wake up in a country that sanctions torture."

"We're all just writing about ourselves," I say.

Nick tells me about a man he's going to see in Turkey, a prisoner from Abu Ghraib, the man Lynndie England appeared to be pulling from his cell on a leash. He says when he talks to people

about torture they often respond, "But they're trying kill us."
"Who?" he says. "Who's trying to kill us?"

I tell Nick about Sean and the Hans Reiser trial. It's been almost two months since I first heard about Sean. I say there's no
body and the man that the victim left her husband for confessed
to eight murders. I tell him all the ways I know Sean. Nick says it
sounds complicated.

"Do you think Sean did it?" Nick asks.

"I don't know," I say. "Sean told my friend Josh that if he
understood Sean's relationship with Hans, Josh would weep piss
and blood."

"Who talks like that?"

I tell Nick I thought I would get to know Sean. Figure him out.
But he disappeared on me and now I'm remembering all these
things I thought I left behind.

The cafés are filled with struggling actors whispering to themselves. A belt of greenish smog lies like spilled sewage across the
mountain range barreling the city. It's different from San Francisco
where the air is clean and the city is beautiful. Los Angeles is big
and ugly. Uglier even than Oakland. Sometimes, in the early evening, Bearman, Nick, and I play basketball at a school yard on the
edge of Hollywood, hoisting our shots with both hands toward
the naked rims. There's never anyone around to see our awkward
athletic display.

"I'm writing for *Esquire*," I tell the paparazzi at the jail where
Paris Hilton is serving time. What else would I say? That I'm waiting for a murder trial to start, sleeping on someone's couch, and
starring in porn films in the San Fernando Valley?

I talk to the inmates as they leave the jail for treatment facilities. One woman is missing her front teeth, top and bottom. The
other had four earrings ripped out during a gang fight in South
Central. She says she was defending her sister.

The PR machine works overtime to flag the story that Paris is serving extra time because she's a celebrity. It's inaccurate but there's nothing to do about it. Paris is given a special bed in the hospital unit. "You have to be dying to get one of those beds," one of the inmates tells me. I pen an editorial pointing out that this is actually about prison crowding and a justice system that works differently for the rich. After a thousand words I'm done.

The night Paris is scheduled to get out I'm with a crowd of journalists flanking the walkway leading from the main entrance, kept back by yellow tape.

"I want pictures of a happy lady," says Nick Ut. Thirty-five years ago he photographed a naked girl running in front of a black cloud, arms spread so as not to touch her sides, 80 percent of her body covered in napalm. In front of the girl, a boy with his mouth open in a black square screams. Behind her, soldiers walk casually, their helmets in place, guns across their shoulders. That pic-

ture won the Pulitzer Prize and helped end a war an ocean away. More recently Ut photographed Paris Hilton crying in the backseat of a police car after being told she was to return to jail.

"You look at the pictures," Nick says. "They're very similar. Also different. Kim was poor and her family suffered a long time. Paris was in jail for three days."

When Paris was first sentenced she said she hoped the media would focus more on the war. When the judge ordered her back, she screamed, "Mom, it's not fair." In a phone interview from jail she said, "It's like being in a cage."

There are hundreds of journalists, a dozen police, and tourists coming in. I meet Ashley Moore, who spent seven days here back in September. She couldn't make bail so she sat in the jail for a week. After she was released the judge dropped the case. She has the Japanese symbol for beautiful on her arm, a rose tattooed on her foot. "That place," she says pointing to the jail, "is no place to be." But here she is, waiting to see Paris get out. She says she has nothing else to do on a Monday night.

As it gets closer to midnight the crowd swells. The TV reporters report live. Helicopters hover overhead. The parents pull up in a large black SUV. Their bodyguard is a big, bald man in a well-tailored suit. He seems to know the police. He looks like he could have been a football player once. The driver wears mirrored glasses and doesn't smile. More tape is stretched to secure the crowd. The thrum of the helicopters is like a soundtrack.

"You're so beautiful, Kathy," a girl cries. The girl looks Spanish or Asian, or both. She's wearing a tank top, her breasts pushed up.

"Thank you," Kathy Hilton says. Kathy sits in the car, the window rolled down, bantering with the press. She soaks the cameras' flashes in like lotion, plays with her hair.

Then the girl says it again, "You're so beautiful, Kathy."

Kathy smiles.

Then the girl says it again and Kathy looks ahead uncomfortably.

"Oh God, please let Paris go free!" a deranged man wails, stretching his arms and dropping to his knees.

Arc lights are set up. It's midnight and everything shines. The reporters lean over the tape. The paparazzi wait with cameras strapped over their necks. All of it infused with the nervous energy of a bull waiting for a clown to unhinge the gate.

And then she is out. Paris Hilton in tight jeans and a light jacket thrown over a white shirt. She's smiling, basking in the glow. She looks better without makeup. She gets to the car and is hugging her mother and then the door is open and she is inside and the tape and the barricades go down and the police cannot control the crowd. The car inches away. The paparazzi stand shins against the bumper, bent across the hood, taking pictures through the glass. Nick Ut stands in the wreckage of toppled tripods left by the young photographers, reviewing pictures he took. He's a little man and this is not exactly his game. But Paris was smiling and happy, exactly as he had hoped.

At four in the morning my phone rings. I flip the bright screen while Bearman's cats look up from the corner. It's my friend Roger, calling from Chicago. Two men jumped him while he was trying to hail a cab. "Oh Steve," he says. "They wouldn't stop." They kept beating him, even after they got his wallet and left him lying in the street almost unconscious. I stay on the phone with Roger for a long time. I talk to the doctor who put five stitches in Roger's face and assures me everything is going to be OK. Later Roger says he just wishes he hadn't been drunk at the time. He would have fought back.

Roger's my oldest friend. I've known him since I was seven. Once, Justin's father pulled up on the sidewalk in his taxi and I took off running. He poked a gun in Roger's chest and asked where I had gone and Roger responded he didn't know. Another time my father caught Roger climbing in through my bedroom window. He stood there with a hammer, considering whether or not to break Roger's fingers. He told me later he was glad he hadn't.

I spend an afternoon at the glassy ocean out at Venice Beach.

There are concrete benches and tables on the beach, an outdoor gym, an ice-cream shop. People are roller-skating up and down the boardwalk. Old men walk in shorts with their shirts off, their bellies toasted by the sun. I think about the difference between being famous and disappearing. Los Angeles is a fantastic place to disappear. There are so many people trying to be recognized that all you have to do is stand still. In the hundreds of miles of sprawling suburbs a person could do nothing here and the time would pass and that would be that.

Hans Reiser's trial won't start for six more weeks, presuming it's not continued, and Sean is still missing. I wonder who else Sean is hiding from, how far he is in over his head. I study the pictures I posed for inside Sean's apartment. I have them in a file on my computer. There are large black tiles on the floor, a plaster angel on the wall in what looks like the entryway, a standing brass lamp and dark wood dresser. I'm tied into a body harness, wearing a blindfold and a spiked collar. A woman in a latex catsuit is posing to look as if she is digging her nails into my face. It was the summer of 1999, right around the time Hans and Nina were getting married on an Oakland hilltop. In the wedding video they dance behind a minotaur and Hans cannot keep his hands off Nina. He grasps for her like a greedy child, the way I

grasped for Lissette. Sean was there dressed in drag, the maid of honor, witnessing for his friend. While I was chained up in his apartment was he already coveting his best friend's wife?

Before I leave Los Angeles I meet a music producer. She asks what I'm working on and I say I am kind of writing a book about murder and kind of not doing anything. She says she tried to kill her stepfather once. She was sixteen and working in a pharmacy and she found a type of pill and figured out how many pills it would take to kill a person. She stole the pills, slipping a couple in her pockets every day, careful to cover her tracks. The night she decided she'd had enough she ground the pills and put them in her stepfather's food.

"Nothing happened," she says. "He was too fat. It went right through his system. He didn't even notice."

Chapter 4

July; Scooter and Eva; Miranda Leaves; The Stranger;
Clues, Rumors, and Observations; What's in Portland;
Kay's Advice; Norman Mailer; The Situation and the
Story; Sean Sturgeon Returns with a Message

In the beginning of July, George Bush commutes Lewis "Scooter" Libby's sentence of thirty months for perjury. He doesn't pardon Libby, who served as the vice president's chief of staff, just changes the sentence so he doesn't serve any time. He says the penalty was too severe but makes no move to change the mandatory sentencing for everyone else. Below the article is a story about Eva Daley, who drove her son and six of his friends to a gang fight in Long Beach where they stabbed a boy to death. It must have looked like a circus trick, all those children piling out of the car toward the playground.

When I get home from Los Angeles I see Miranda in the afternoon and we make a large pot of curried vegetables. I don't see her again until a week later when her roommates are having a party and she asks to sleep over. She has to be up at four in the morning to go to work. She says she's been busy. She says she's having an existential crisis. She met a boy at a rock show and thinks maybe she's in love. She's wearing tennis shoes, a sweatshirt, and yellow running shorts. We walk down Cortland looking for ice cream but all the shops are closed.

Miranda is tired. The work she's doing is secret, possibly illegal, and justified by the causes she represents. She doesn't go to movies or watch television. She reads essays to support her desires, reinforces her beliefs with books like *Is Multiculturalism Bad for Women?* At night she closes herself around me while I lean over the side of the bed with the covers pushed back, sweating. Miranda's legs pressed behind my legs feel like they're a hundred degrees. I'm trying not to panic. I wake up startled in the middle of the night and she lays her hand over my face, spreading her fingers across my eyes.

"Go back to sleep," she says. "You belong to me."

In the morning her clothes are gone, along with her bag of books, her bicycle. I put on the mix CD she made while I cook eggs and make coffee.

I'm moving soon. Just a little more than a mile away into a one-bedroom apartment with a twenty-six-year-old kid who works for a guitar magazine. I tap my pen on the table and stare past the fire escape, contemplating the hill. I hear a series of explosions behind the building. It's the Fourth of July.

"You're twitching," my psychiatrist says. "Above your eye."

"I've always had a twitch," I say.

When I was younger I could barely control it. I would roll my lips, blink quickly, nod my head in short, quick jerks. I was so tense I could only wear extra-large clothes that hung on me like sacks because I couldn't stand the feeling of fabric pressing my shoulders. She says the Adderall could make it worse. She asks if I want to start taking medication for depression. She suggests Welbutrin or a serotonin agent.

"I don't know," I say. "I don't think I want to be on any more pills."

I tell her I took Paxil once but it just made things worse. My father, I suspect, also suffers from depression. A deep sadness always followed his rage. "I'm awful," he would say after his fits. There might be broken plates across the kitchen floor and he would be standing in my doorway, the bags beneath his eyes heavy with grief. He would offer a gift, like a bowl of ice cream or a glass of Coke. "I feel terrible about it." That was his way of talking about things. His apologies always came with an assurance that he was hurting too, that he could be trusted to take care of his own punishments. He needed to know I forgave him, as if he couldn't go on otherwise. But I knew he would erupt again, exploding through the house like a thunderstorm, and I didn't have any forgiveness in me.

When I got older we patched things up for a while but it didn't work out. I haven't spoken to my father in a long time. Our last real conversation was an argument over the phone in 2004. I was writing a book about the presidential election and I could see Pennsylvania senator Arlen Specter nearby at the entrance to a veteran's hospital. My novel *Happy Baby* was just out. As in all of my novels, the protagonist is a stand-in for me. He was raised in group homes and was heavily into S/M. It was my first time writing honestly about my sexual desires and my tendency to eroticize my childhood.

I received a note from a journalist who, after interviewing me, had been contacted by my father. My father told him I was a liar, a spoiled child from an upper-middle-class home looking for attention. He told him that I could have come home at any time, which wasn't true; when I was arrested at age fourteen I didn't know where he lived. My father disputed basic facts, saying I had gone to two high schools, not four. That I left home at fifteen, not thirteen. He didn't shave my head, he gave me a haircut. He only handcuffed me to a pipe one time, he said, and look how many stories I wrote about it. It didn't take long to realize this wasn't the first journalist my father had contacted. He left a trail of denials across the internet like digital breadcrumbs.

Everywhere I found a review of the book I would also find his comments.

"What's wrong with you?" I asked. I was incredulous. There was the senator in front of me, his arm wrapped around a soldier whose leg had been amputated below the knee, and I was sitting in the parking lot and couldn't even get out of the car.

"I know, son, I know," my father said, as if he felt sorry for me.

My writer's block began after that conversation. I had based my identity on a year spent sleeping on the streets and the four years that followed. It wasn't much of a foundation. He was questioning my story, telling anyone who would listen that I had made up the whole thing, my entire life. I began to qualify everything. I wouldn't say anything about myself without first saying there were people who remembered things differently. I wondered how much I had mythologized my own history, arranged my experiences to highlight my successes and excuse my failures. How far had I strayed from the truth?

When I stopped responding to my father he pushed further. Yes, he wrote, he had yelled quite a bit and maybe, since my room was off the kitchen, I had mistakenly thought he was yelling at me. Then the group homes became foster homes and finally I had never even been in a foster home, I wouldn't know what one looked like, everything was the product of my imagination, a result perhaps of something that happened in the mental hospital in 1986. He was trying to obliterate me. He was stealing my past and I was trying to hold on but felt it slipping through my fingers. I started to disappear.

In the documents from Read Mental Hospital, a doctoral psychology student writes, *Stephen experiences interpersonal relationships as unsatisfying and leave him with feelings of loneliness and isolation. His family system is not experienced as a haven where warmth and nurturance are demonstrated. Paternal figures are seen as punitive and rejecting. Maternal figures are seen in more positive light but are unavailable resulting in feeling of abandonment* (sic). That was more than twenty years ago. I get the notes my father sends through reviews or comments almost every month telling me I need to apologize to my dead mother. I hear from female writers who my father has written to. "I liked your article. I think you know my son . . ." Growing up he would flirt with my friends' mothers. He once offered to get an apartment for a girlfriend of mine. "A girl that pretty shouldn't have to work." I see the mean reviews he leaves of my books on Amazon. And I think, I don't need antidepressants. I have real problems.

I'm sitting on a black chair with my feet up, staring at my psychiatrist scratching notes on the digital tablet on her lap. It costs me $75 a visit, more for the meds. Each visit is only fifteen minutes long. She has so much faith in her pills; she doesn't know me at all. I wish we could go for a walk and I could try to explain some of it to her. I wish we could sit for three hours on top of Bernal Heights. I think she would have good advice. She's wearing a long black dress, her hair piled in a bun on her head. She's a nice lady. She's getting ready to retire and the lines on her face are rivulets of empathy. I'm twitching. She's telling me I should take antidepressants and I'm thinking of Tolstoy saying the only conclusion a reasonable person can come to is that life is meaningless. And then everything seems like a cliché.

I pay my doctor and head outside where I'm reminded of something else: the sun greeting Meursault in Camus' *The Stranger*. Meursault fails to show remorse at his mother's funeral and then, at the beach, takes one step forward when he knows he should take one step back, and is blinded by the light flashing off the Arab's blade.

I can't find Sean but I find more than a dozen people who know him. Sean wanted to turn his dungeon studio into a church so that all the dominatrixes who worked there would be priestesses, safeguarded by laws protecting religious freedoms. "He's like that," someone says. "He's always looking for an angle."

Several people remember Sean claiming he murdered someone as long as ten years ago.

"Why didn't you go to the police?" I ask one person.

"I didn't believe him," that person says.

Everybody seems to have a different opinion of Sean. They often refer to his generosity and kindness. One person says if Sean claims to have killed eight people then it's true. Sean's not a liar. Others caution me to keep my distance.

"What do you mean?" I ask.

"He's hard to get rid of. Once he's in your life he won't want to go away. He sees it as a game."

I also hear something more disturbing. Someone says Sean called a friend just weeks before Nina disappeared. The friend described Sean as extremely agitated, saying Sean couldn't understand how Nina could leave him and why she was refusing to see him.

I go to Portland for a writers' workshop at Reed College. Every day I read work by my ten students and we sit around a coffee table discussing their essays. One woman says she's an abuse survivor, another writes about a car crash she survived but in which her boyfriend died. One writes about doing her MFA in New York and how one of the students stole a story idea from another student and published it in a book. A man from Iowa says the class is really just an excuse to visit his grandchildren. He's seventy-four years old and once ran for Congress. One morning he asks if anyone read the local paper. "This young woman," he says. "She was killed over in Iraq. Shot by a sniper. Now her two kids have no mother. And we're sitting around talking about where to put a fucking period."

As part of the conference I give a reading at an outdoor amphitheater with rows of white wood benches leading up to the Gray Campus Center. It's a quiet evening with fifty students and faculty sitting patiently while I read an essay about Lissette carving "possession" in my side. She spelled it wrong, leaving out one *s*. The metaphor was too obvious. It was like Jim Morrison dying in the bathtub or Ronald Reagan's tax cuts. It meant exactly what you thought it meant.

In Los Angeles, Bearman had told me I needed to find a new story. I had written four novels based loosely on my life and multiple personal essays. "Listen," he said. "Stick to Hans and Sean and keep yourself out of it." My friend Kay encourages me to write something accessible, and to keep a journal for the rest. "Write something that people want to read," she says. "Think of Dave Eggers. He wrote a book about himself and moved on to other things." Twelve years ago, when I was hospitalized following my overdose, my friend Louie came to visit me. He said, "You better never write about this." He was trying to distinguish between being a real human being and someone who only lives on the page. I didn't even consider myself a writer then, though I wrote all the time.

I was in the hospital for eight days after my overdose. My body was covered in strange boils and for most of my time there I could barely move. I had a stroke, or a seizure. The doctors didn't know and didn't seem to care. My troubles were self-inflicted.

I checked out early, returning to the room I rented on the third floor of a large house near the university, walking with a limp. Suddenly I noticed how yellow the walls were, and how the roof rose at a sharp angle, cutting the space in half. I stopped eating. I lost twenty-five pounds. I couldn't focus and I began to have panic attacks, which I hadn't experienced since I was in the group homes.

Soon after leaving the hospital I began to fantasize about getting a gun and going to the lake and putting the gun in my mouth and toppling back into the water. I would kill myself just like Kurt Cobain had two years earlier. But it was winter, and I worried that the frozen lake would keep me alive and I would be rescued somehow. It was all I could think about. A month after I was out of the hospital I showed up back at the emergency room and told them what I was going to do. A resident gave me some Klonopin and sent me home. The next day I enrolled in a drug treatment program.

My friends think I'm a happy person. And in a way I am. But I've been sad a lot too. When I'm sad I don't want anyone to know. I try to hide it, even from myself. I read books on depression. They all say to take your meds; it's a matter of finding the right cocktail. But the authors also talk about recurrences, shifting dosages, sleeping ten hours a night, and losing all interest in sex. It's only recently that I'm realizing I've been depressed all my life. I run from it like a fire. I could stand under a thousand spotlights, publish a million books, and it wouldn't change a thing.

At the end of the Portland conference I stand outside the main hall with one of the students. She's a lawyer, educated at Yale. She used her vacation to come here. I want to go inside, talk to some of the people I met. But the student is so beautiful. She says the faculty are like celebrities.

"Why are you talking to me?" she asks. "I'm too boring for you. I'm not going to carve 'possession' over your ribs."

I imagine her knife sliding inside me, cutting along my stomach, peeling back my skin. She leans against the wall, playing with her hair.

"Maybe I'm trying to get to the other side of that," I tell her.

Her shirt is unbuttoned. Her skin is dark and smooth. "You like exotic women," she says. "And you're attracted to things you can't have." She leans toward me, like a dare. I press my hand on her waist and kiss her, lingering against her lips. She says she has a boyfriend. Someone her mother would like. I am not someone her mother would like. She's been trying to please her mother her entire life.

When I get back from Portland, Miranda informs me she doesn't want to see me for a while. Her life is in turmoil. It has nothing to do with me. We just sleep together. We were just acting as placeholders for each other. Anyway, I had my chance.

I think about Norman Mailer rewriting *The Deer Park* in a Benzedrine haze, popping Seconal to find some sleep at night and waking in a stupor. Benzedrine and Adderall are essentially the same thing. Mailer was the biggest literary star of his time, but *The Deer Park* was not a great book. Later he would remember, *"I would pick up the board, wait for the first sentence—like all working addicts I had come to an old man's fine sense of inner timing—and then slowly, but picking up speed, the actions of the drugs hovering into collaboration like two ships passing in view of one another, I would work for an hour, not well but not badly either. Then my mind would wear out, and new work was done for the day. I would sit around, watch more television and try to rest my dulled mind, but by evening a riot of bad nerves was on me again, and at two in the morning I'd be having the manly debate of whether to try to sleep with two double capsules, or settle again for my need of three.*"[8] He describes my life perfectly, except when he wrote this he had already made something of himself. Much later he would write his true crime masterpiece, *The Executioner's Song*, which gives me hope. He wrote his best book years after his TV and pills and marijuana, his thirties behind him. When asked what five novels he would bring with him to a desert island, he said his own.

I think about calling my father. I have so many questions. What was the man's name? Did he really kill him? Did he sleep with my mother's sister or was he joking? Does he still have pictures of himself from after the men beat him up? Can I see them? What were the names of the books he gave me to read? Why did he want to be a writer in the first place? Who was Al Capone's lawyer? How do you bore holes in a shotgun? I just want the facts.

Sitting on top of Dolores Park hill with a friend, I mention I'm working on a new book. She asks what it's about.

"I'm writing about murder," I tell her. I have no more classes scheduled, no income coming in. The memoirist Vivian Gornick would say the murder is just the situation; the story is something else.

It's golden hour, the sun is down and everything is evenly lit. The park is filled with couples making out.

And then Sean returns.

It's been months since I last heard from him. We meet at a diner in the Castro. He sits in front of a wall of bright posters of the Jersey Boys, Bob Marley, MenInGear.com. We're at a long table. It's ten at night. Men pass the windows in Day-Glo tank tops and tight pants.

What Sean most wants to tell me is that my friend Josh may be

---

8. Norman Mailer, *Advertisements for Myself* (Putnam, 1959), 244.

in danger. He says he heard friends of Hans didn't like the article. "These are bad people," he says. "Just try to think: who would still be friends with Hans?" *(Who would still be friends with a murderer?)* He says I should tell Josh to look out.

I shrug my shoulders and order a bowl of chili. He didn't like the article and he wants me to scare someone on his behalf. He's manipulative but clumsy. He mentions the article again.

"Nobody ever likes what's written about them," I snap. I name a couple of books he could read on the subject. I mention Janet Malcolm, who referred to being written about as having a sort of narcissist's holiday but who also said that when the holiday was over and the article or book has been published, the subject had the experience of flunking a test she didn't know she was taking.[9]

Sean's upset because in the article Josh called him evasive.

"You *are* evasive," I say. "I've interviewed politicians. You are the most evasive person I've ever met."

"That's because I don't even know you," he says. I don't say that he contacted me this time. That I had given up on trying to meet with him when he disappeared and turned off his phone. That I don't trust him because he answers questions with questions, tells stories with analogies rather than facts, converses in detail about everything except what interests me. He says he grew up in a commune but I don't know the commune's name. For all I know it wasn't a commune at all. Maybe it was just a normal house where a lot of people stopped by. All I know about him is that on Sundays he goes to church and that he loved a woman and that woman is gone.

"I don't mean it as an insult," I say. But maybe I do. Maybe

---

9. Janet Malcolm, *The Journalist and the Murderer* (New York: Vintage, 1990).

what I really want to say is, Why are you doing this? Why are you wasting my time? Why are you leading me into this rabbit hole?

"I'm going to help you with your book," he says. "But I can't talk to you about it until after the trial."

"By that time I don't know what I'll be writing about," I say. "Anyway, you wouldn't like how it turned out. You wouldn't like how I portrayed you."

I ask Sean how he is doing and he looks at me like I'm crazy. He was attacked a second time, he says. He lives in a condo in the East Bay and someone broke into the garage. He heard feet scampering and then someone hit him in the back of the head with a pipe and he passed out.

"I didn't see them." He says there were things pertaining to Nina missing from his car, and other things. I say it could be unrelated. He says he'll be curious to see what evidence suddenly appears at the trial. Why would he have evidence related to Nina in his car? He wants to know what I've been doing. I tell him about standing outside the jail when Paris Hilton was released, the seminar in Portland. I tell him about making the gossip pages in the *San Francisco Chronicle* by throwing a beer on a sixty-six year-old man at a literary event.[10]

"I couldn't live the kind of life you lead," he says. He likes quiet, says the police requested that he turn in his guns. I thought he gave his guns to his pastor. "I've never shot anyone," he says. "I've been shot at once. They should have taken my knives."

The restaurant is crowded, noisy, and overlit. Sean's hinting that at least some of the people he killed were killed with knives, which would make for one hell of a mess. The boys are filtering into the diner from the gay bars. "I was supporting Nina even though she was with another man," Sean says. He's drinking a

---

10. Leah Garchik, *San Francisco Chronicle*, July 20, 2007.

mimosa. He says Nina was about to take the first round of the medical boards. "If she passed she would be able to get a better job." He starts crying, the tears rolling gently down his nose.

I don't feel the sympathy I'm supposed to feel. I feel empty. I wonder if the Adderall is making me cold, or if it's just the lack of sleep. It makes me think of my own mother and how I didn't cry when she died. Instead I went with some friends down to the canal and we drank a bottle of vodka. I was thirteen. "Drink to forget," Nicko said. I didn't cry for years.

I fold my hands and watch Sean's face. I asked him once about the people left behind, the children, the lovers. He said that wasn't his concern. I could see from his expression that he had never even considered it. If he did kill those people, he hadn't given a thought to the collateral damage. He didn't care. The murderer crying because he has lost the woman he loves to a killer. Is he crying for himself or for Nina or the two children? How could he feel remorse but not guilt? What does "loss" mean? How do we convince ourselves of loss? Nina had already left him. He was still giving her money though she hadn't seen him in four months. It's not that his pain isn't real, just unknowable. It belongs to him, exists in the complex forge of his heart. The words and the tears are the product of this engine but they don't communicate anything. I'm blind to what's inside.

At the same time I'm talking to Sean, an old friend of mine is placing a loaded gun in his mouth. Six weeks ago Mike fell and cracked his skull while visiting a doctor for strep throat. Since then he'd been having panic attacks, ringing in his ears, and depression. He may have been there that night at the canal after my mother died. He usually was. Once he was just another stoned kid, like the rest of us, like Tom, who died a couple of years ago on his drug dealer's floor, flopping like a fish while his dealer searched the internet for a way to revive him. Or Rich Herrera, who last year followed a three-day coke binge with a handful of sleeping pills, stopping his heart. Mike had been doing well. He had a wife and a child. He was a police officer, a profession that seems to attract juvenile criminals, at least in the Chicago area. Mike pulls the trigger, blows out the back of his head.

I get the phone call about Mike from Roger two days later while in the terminal at SFO waiting for a plane to New York. I'm supposed to give a reading at the Museum of Sex in Manhattan. I'm sitting by the window, looking at a flight boarding for Indonesia, a sky blue Korean Air jet taxiing the runway. Then the tarmacs and the bay followed by the hills. I tell Roger I have to go, my flight's boarding, though it isn't actually boarding for another hour. There've been a lot of these calls in the past few years. I'm missing everybody's funeral.

But I don't know about Mike yet, the taste of gun like a mouthful of coins, his wife, five months pregnant with a second child, stopping in front of the door with no idea what awaits her inside.

I'm sitting across from a man who may be a murderer, but I can't tell. "I need to leave the life of violence behind me," Sean says as the waitress takes his empty bowl and refills my water. "I just can't handle all the things I'm doing. There's no winners in this. Everybody loses."

CHAPTER 5

Late July/Early August; Goldberg's Funeral; A Prostitute on Victoria Avenue; Ted Light Shoots a Homeless Man with a Crossbow; Risk and Reward; The Coast of Chicago; Arriving in San Francisco; A Real Job with Benefits

In a funeral home on the Northwest Side of Chicago, Mike lies in an open casket, five days dead, his bloated face covered in thick makeup. He looks like a large doll. I stand at the back of the room near the heavy drapes. Mike's daughter is there on the couch with her chin on her tiny fists watching a small DVD player. A detail of Columbia, Missouri's police department is in attendance in their dress blues. One of the officers who worked with Mike tells me that rookies would sometimes ask Mike to identify the drugs they'd found, and we laugh. Mike never had any problem identifying drugs. "He was a good guy," the officer says. Just like that.

After the wake there's the funeral. It's raining. A rabbi speaks while a lady in a smart suit holds an umbrella above him. We take turns shoveling dirt onto the casket. "That costs $150," Javier says, pointing to a square of white flowers on top of a grave. He used to work in the cemetery. "Plus maintenance." Mike's mother is here. His home situation wasn't as bad as most of ours. Both his parents were alive, though separated. Mike's father invites everyone over to his house for food but we go to a bar instead.

We don't talk a lot about Mike, who was a nice guy and didn't get in much trouble. We talk about Tim Strutz and his Camaro fishtailing through the alleys near Devon. I mention that I was volunteering in a homeless shelter my senior year in high school when Tim came in on the other side of the line. Someone mentions Tomlee taking the police on a high-speed chase and then, surrounded in a parking lot, refusing to get out of the car and the police punching him repeatedly in the head while he sat in the driver's seat. Ant was out of the car and standing with his arms folded across his chest while Tomlee got his beating. "Are you scared?" the cop asked him.

"No," Ant said. "I'm just cold."

We talk about the house burglary ring Aaron started in 1986. Aaron wasn't at Mike's funeral today. He once told me he started robbing houses because he wanted to be like me. I had just returned from hitchhiking to California and he said he wanted to have stories to tell too. He spent years in jail. Last time I saw him he was shooting up in his apartment. "Yeah," he said. "I'm a junky." It didn't bother him. He stuck the needle right in his leg. He sold me my last bundle of heroin, ten poorly mixed bags including a hotshot full of pure juice that nearly killed me.

"Where is that guy, anyway?" Roger asks.

Ant orders sandwiches and pitchers of beer. We talk about the kids that came in from the suburbs. They'd brought a keg down to the canal and didn't want to share. They didn't know they were in our space, that we had dug the fire pit and made the stairs and slept many nights there while the rats ducked in and out of the muck. There were more of them than us and the largest stood in front of Ron Fessedon and said, "It's time for you guys to leave." Ron got a queer look on his face then pulled a branch from the tree and punched him in the temple with it and he fell face-first in the dirt, his girlfriend screaming, "You killed him!" Everybody scattered.

Eddie mentions Billy showing up drunk and losing his job at UPS. Roger remembers Mitch taking off his shirt at Eddie's wedding, Pat throwing a bottle through the window of Devon Bank. Javier talks about coming home to his first apartment and seeing a trail of blood in the hallway and hoping it didn't lead to his door, but of course it did. His roommate was covered in bandages, sitting in a straight-backed chair. He'd been fighting with his girlfriend and glass was everywhere.

When we get together these are always the stories we tell. Stories of theft and violence. We tell the same stories over and over again and I always learn something new. This time I learn that the decision to rob Paul's parents' house was made in my father's car, which Tim McKitrick had stolen that morning. My father used to attach a set of magnetic keys to the underside of the bumper. I don't remember telling anybody about them, but I probably did.

"There were an unusual number of sociopaths in our group," Roger observes. "Including your father."

It's true, I think. We're proud of our stories. They make us sound tougher than we were. Actually we were weak and rarely stood up for one another. We had no group identity and no sense of loyalty. We weren't into anything except bad heavy metal music, and a lot of us weren't even into that, we were just faking it. We rooted against each other and maintained no rituals other than getting high. I was also a thief. Crawling into my parents' room late at night, dragging my father's pants along the floor then rummaging through his pockets, trying to decide how much money I could take without him noticing. He always had bail money, up to a $1,000 in cash, and I would take $200 or $300 at a time. The year before my mother died I must have stolen $2,000. I remember my heart beating so hard and fast I was worried it would shake the furniture. And I remember the bright bathroom lights at four in the morning, the blood drained from my face, leaning against the sink trying to control my breathing as I waited for the lump in my throat to subside. I remember dragging the pants back into their room. And the staggering quantities of drugs I would buy with that money.

A lot of my friends are living at home again with their parents, getting into their late thirties, still trying to figure it out. It's too late for most of us. A few are doing well. Alex owns his own computer support business. Roger is completing a PhD in psychology. Ant is a contractor, happily married with a gorgeous child, selling rebuilt classic cars on the side. Dave, Rob, and Pat play in bands. There are no CEOs, no VPs of marketing. Justin's back home more than twenty years after the state took custody of him, sleeping in the same room where his father beat him with a stick. Javier is nearing forty, intermittently homeless.

"There weren't many women in our group when we were younger," Javier points out.

"Can you blame them?" I reply.

The drinking continues until late when Velchry, stumbling drunk, can't find his car. We end up at the RedLine Tap watching the neighborhood bluegrass band, and then I leave and walk down the cobblestone street next to the Morse Station. The last train clatters past overhead. Mike is dead. It doesn't make any sense, compared with some of the people still alive. Velchry has a child he rarely sees. So does Eddie. Dave and Nadia split custody. Justin has a child with his ex-wife. Bob moved back into the city while his wife is in the suburbs with their two children. We've bred children into broken homes. The next generation of ourselves. I pass the No Exit Cafe, where I used to play chess with the off-duty cabdrivers. I was a good player. After I convinced the group home to send me to the normal high school my junior year, I joined the chess team and came in sixth in the city. The principal made an announcement over the intercom.

A woman calls to me from the end of the street. "Hey," she says. "Can you help me out?" It's two in the morning. She wears a thin synthetic shirt, the straps hanging loosely, lines of sweat running down her arms. She reminds me of a prostitute on Victoria Avenue, not far away. She was the first woman who treated me the way I wanted. She wanted more money than I had . . .

A man in a white T-shirt wants to talk to me about something. He's holding the corner with two other men. He has a scraggly halo of a beard. "I'm talking to you," he says. "Hey, man. I'm talking to you." The lights are on in front of JB's, the delivery drivers double-parked to the end of the block. It's the best pizza in America but if you stop for a slice late at night you don't know what's going to happen. The tiny strip mall with the hair salon and Magic Video is closed for the night. I want to tell the hustlers and hookers and crackheads that I grew up here and went to public schools. If I hadn't left they would recognize me, and instead of asking me for something or motioning to me with their fingers or calling out, "What you want? What you need?" they would just nod. If I had never left, then I could walk safely past the white shirts between the bar and my friend's house with the futon in the living room four blocks away, and these people would be there to guarantee my safe passage. And occasionally I would give them a beer from a six-pack I was taking home and occasionally they would ask if I would like a drink and we would share a bottle across from the bus stop and talk about where the neighborhood is going, the new grocery store on Howard, the shuttered post office. But I left and not everybody recognizes me now.

I stay near the lake in what's known as East Rogers Park. It's an area that's almost equally black, white, and Hispanic. When the lost boys started arriving from the Sudan, they landed in East Rogers Park. Towards Ridge, where the Kurds emigrated when Saddam Hussein came to power in the eighties, the store signs are written in Arabic. Then West Rogers Park, the strip along Devon known as Little India, where traffic drags to a halt, the street crowded with spice vendors and sari shops. Then the small

Orthodox enclave on the other side of California, formerly the entry point for Russian Jews during Operation Exodus, most of whom have moved to suburbs. There's also a small community of religious Koreans and a new wave of East Europeans fresh from the Balkan wars. Rogers Park has always been this way. It has to be among the most diverse neighborhoods in the country. Between the Kurds and the Indians is the state park and the Jiffy Lube on Western Avenue, the longest street in the city. Four blocks west of that is CSC, the special school for group home kids and children with behavior disorders that I attended when I was fifteen.

The school was four floors with steel doors and buzzer locks on the outside. The teachers were kind and there were only six of us in each class but it seemed that every day in that school someone was being restrained. We were just across the street from Mather, the normal high school, a single-story compound with an aluminum-wrapped flat roof, over fifteen hundred students, and its own park. That wasn't a good school either; only 60 percent of the students graduated. I wanted to go there. The Mather students slouched past our windows in the morning with no idea they were passing us by.

Near the school was Green Briar Park where we played basketball. It was also the hangout for a gang called the Popes, as well as for a local drug dealer named Ted Light. Ted was two years older than I was, with a smooth, fat face. He wore polo shirts and looked like he was from somewhere else. I didn't know anyone who dressed like him. Once, when we were picking up drugs at his house and he had left the room, Nicko lifted Ted's bedding to show the rubber sheet underneath. Ted was a bed wetter.

Ted owned a crossbow and he used it to shoot small animals climbing telephone poles in his alley. One day Ted and a twenty-seven-year-old car thief named Dwight Lambert drove toward the lake, then south, past the fancy buildings in Lincoln Park. They took the ramp near the river onto Lower Wacker Drive where the trucks came in the morning full of furniture and clothing bound for Chicago's department stores. Ted spotted a homeless man in a loading dock, sleeping on his left side on top of a cardboard box. Dwight idled the car while Ted pulled on a pair of leather gloves, slid a serrated razor-tipped arrow into the bow, aimed from the window, and shot the man in the heart. The man flipped onto his back, mouth wide, gasping for air as his heart seized and his body released his ghost. The two men waited, like children at an aquarium, watching him die before Ted took off his gloves, stored the crossbow, and drove away.

"You know the killer instinct?" Ted asked Eddie a couple of days later. They were smoking Ted's pot as he explained how the man flopped onto his back after the arrow plunged into his chest. "Everyone wants to know what it's like to take another man's life."

Four years later, after being found guilty of murdering Gaylord Tolbert, Ted told Cook County judge Earl Strayhorn, "I'm not an evil person. My face may not show it, but my heart is filled with sorrow." Then he was led to the holding cell where he met Javier.

"How'd it go?" Javier asked.

"They gave me sixty years," Ted replied.

There were more than fifty men in that cell and Ted sat on the floor like an affectless Buddha.

"He didn't seem to care. Maybe he was relieved," Javier said.

Javier would do six months waiting for his own trial for criminal property damage. His girlfriend had turned him in for grave robbing. Ironic, since he would one day maintain the cemetery grounds. None of us were able to come up with the $5,000 necessary to bail him out. We didn't even try.

At a bar watching a friend's band two days after Mike's funeral I ask Eddie about the $1,000 reward for information that led to Ted Light's arrest. Eddie shakes his head and mentions being exploited in my writing before. People often feel exploited when they find themselves in my work. It doesn't matter if I call it fiction; I know as well as they do that's not an excuse. I don't bother trying to defend myself. It's not defensible, it's just what I do. I spend years crafting a two-hundred-page story, all the time my life sits next to me like a jar of paint.

I want to tell Eddie that writing a novel is an act of love, but it's much more complicated than that. We're standing outside of a rock club. It's midsummer and Mike is dead. Eddie's trying to rebuild his life. He's lost his license and the mother of his child has taken out a restraining order against him. He says maybe he should get a cut from my writing.

"How about I buy you a beer?" I say.

"That'll work," he replies, though I know it won't.

We spent our entire childhood together. In third grade I punched him in the face. I once created a fake company to get him honorably discharged from the airforce. He almost failed high school in his fifth year and I got up an hour early every day to get him out of bed and drag him to classes. I would give anything to care about somebody that way again. Later he told me that high school was a mistake. He didn't need a diploma. He should have just gone to work. He's the only guy I know who regrets graduating high school.

Before I leave Chicago I grab lunch with Roger. We talk about the times we've pulled apart, inevitable when you've known someone nearly thirty years. But we're closer now than ever. He's the first person I would call in a crisis.

I was seven and playing soccer with my father when we met. My mother said he was an alley kid. A year after I met Roger my mother felt dizzy and went to see a doctor. She was bedridden almost immediately. My father built a ramp up the front stairs for her wheelchair, but she didn't like to go outside sickly and shaking. When I say my mother had multiple sclerosis, people don't know what I mean. They think it's something that comes and goes and stays with you into old age. But that's not what happened. She lost control of her bladder and peed in a bucket next to the couch. I would empty the bucket into the toilet. She shook so hard she could barely lift her head and sat all day watching a small black and white television. I remember wondering why she didn't have a larger TV. She liked Oprah, and the soap operas, and she liked a sitcom called *Benson* about a butler who became the lieutenant governor. She liked the show so much she named our cat, a fat tabby with white paws, Benson.

I was eight when she got sick and thirteen when she died and I can't fully reconstruct what happened between us. I remember telling her I loved her and I remember trying to get affection by saying, "You don't love me anymore." I remember the quilt that covered her those five years. But there's some deep hole in my memory of my mother. There are all these details, but not as many as there should be. I can remember saying things, but not feeling anything. She lay on the couch virtually paralyzed watching that tiny television. I have pictures of my mother, before she was sick and after. I can see how her face became hollow and ghostly, her high cheeks sinking against her jawbones, the redness in her eyes and her lips contrasting sharply with her pallor. I remember her tears, which were cold, running down her cheeks and onto mine as I kissed her and made up another excuse to leave the house.

Roger tells me I've always been good at reinventing myself. I tell him I'm thinking about going on antidepressants. He says he's been on antidepressants for ten years and they've made all the difference. I tell Roger about the Adderall, how I'm ashamed to tell anybody about the pills I'm taking and I don't want to add another one into the mix. I tell him about the murders, the similarities between Sean, my father, and me. I realize this is the first I've mentioned Sean since my plane landed.

"Sean won't talk to me until after Hans' trial."

"What are you going to do?"

"I'm going to go to the trial. See if Hans is guilty. Maybe Sean had nothing to do with it. Maybe he's just some fringe character making up crimes he didn't commit."

"But why would anybody confess to eight murders he didn't commit?"

"I don't know," I say. "But if he killed eight people, or believes he killed eight people, he's crazy either way." *But what if he's lying and he knows it? What if he's just a prankster trying to trick someone into writing a book about him?*

Roger has a scar under his eye from stitches he got after he was mugged not too long ago. I tell him it looks good. He wants to know when I'm coming back and I say I don't have any plans.

Back in those group homes I learned that people come and go. I learned that relationships aren't permanent or guaranteed and I will never be safe. And yet I have all these old friends and we're still in touch years later. Guys who used to ditch high school and motion to me during recess, shaking bags of weed. Guys from the basketball courts, park benches, school steps, rooftops, group homes, and canals of my childhood. I just wish we'd found a way to come up with Javier's bail money. I wish we hadn't robbed each other's houses. I wish we hadn't turned on each other so often. I wish we had rooted for each other. I wish we hadn't let each other down so many times.

I tell Roger I love him very much. "Come out to San Francisco," I say. "It's the most beautiful city in the world."

When I left Chicago in late 1997 I wasn't thinking about San Francisco; I wasn't thinking about anywhere. I wondered where I would end up but felt just a vague, rootless anxiety because I had no idea.

I spent a season in a ski resort high in the Rocky Mountains near the Loveland Pass where you can glide through trees lit by moonlight on a giant thirty-minute ski run in soft, untouched powder. A dozen of us hit the pass on those winter nights. We pushed back from the ridge, hurtling toward the valley, the sky blurry with stars. I would lean back on my board, waving the tip above the surface, snow buzzing my ankles like fairies. It felt like riding a cloud. We sailed through clusters of trees, jumping small creek beds. In the mountains nobody ever asked what

you did for a living or where you were from. At the base, flushed and cold, we'd strap our gear over our shoulders and hike back to the top.

When winter was over and the snow was melting I came down from the mountain. I drove into southern Utah where they film the Nike commercials. I lay on a bench for twelve hours outside the Moab post office trying to decide where to go. I had left my fiancée and the weight of that was finally on me. I was in a part of Utah famed for its sandstone arches and deep gorges, kayakers paddling the rapids that swept up along the pink and brown canyon walls. I kept all my possessions inside my hatchback: snowboard, bicycle, photographs, and several boxes of papers. I considered staying in the Lazy Turtle hostel with a hippie who made her living beading necklaces. Instead I continued on the Nevada 50, the "loneliest road in America," a barren two-lane street across the longest stretch of the state, gas stations and a brothel every fifty miles, listening to Radiohead's *OK Computer* until Reno rose ahead of me in a neon rage.

In San Francisco I slept in my car above the Castro, the seat reclined as far as it would go. I went to the bars and asked men to buy me drinks. I would listen to their problems, acting like a young hustler, the real JT Leroy, except I'd been plucked off the streets years ago. I was better looking than when I was a homeless fourteen-year-old. My skin was clearer, and I was more prepared to strike a deal. But I didn't have much to sell.

One man took me home. He lived on a small street in Twin Peaks. "I shouldn't be doing this," he said. I slept in his spare bedroom, where he kept a wooden cross with eyebolts and leather shackles drilled into the wall.

"If you come home drunk I'm going to chain you to that and fuck you," he said.

"I'd prefer it if you didn't," I replied.

I was twenty-six and I hadn't committed to any city. I had

been crisscrossing the country like a dog chasing his tail and I was in California again. I hadn't spent a year in the same house or apartment since I was thirteen. I thought I was just passing through.

It was a time when people were coming to San Francisco for a reason. Innovators and Ivy Leaguers clogging the entry ramps to the digital age, pulling the levers of the roaring stock market housed in cool server banks throughout the Bay Area. A gold rush was under way. The 101, the primary artery between the city and Silicon Valley, was littered with billboards flashing by like pages of a flipbook advertising Web sites to nowhere. There were private parties every night in the small dark bars in North Beach and South of Market. They were easy to get into and inside everything was free. People talked about "vaporware" and "loss leaders" and "CRM" and the importance of losing money. They carried the next big thing on a disc at the bottom of their backpack. It was more random than a dartboard thrown at a map, but it's where I ended up. Kids my age were billionaires overnight.

I got a job summarizing free catalogs for a database called Catalogs2Go. There was another temp whose only job was to find more free catalogs to order that I could then describe. They came every day, hundreds of them: catalogs for gardening, lawn furniture, fabric distributors, handmade popsicle-stick houses. They sat above and beneath my feet, filling the shelves and window ledge. I tried to paraphrase five an hour, but that became four, and then three. Then I stopped altogether and sat watching the city through the window, all the people sifting between downtown buildings.

After a month I walked into the vice president's office and told him I hadn't done anything in weeks and he didn't know that because he had no system of accountability. I told him I could finish his Web site in ten days. They'd been working on it for almost a year.

"We don't want to hire you," he said.

"I'm not asking you to hire me," I said.

He gave me an office and a phone. I asked people I met at poetry readings to write summaries at $5 a description. The catalogs disappeared and the office became clean and the vice president asked if I would join the company and offered me $50,000 and I let out a low whistle and that was that.

Catalogs2Go was the perfect symbol of the time, a Web site dedicated to giving away something that was already free, but it was just a whim of the vice president, it had nothing to do with the company, and the technical support cost $20,000 a month. There was talk of shutting the Web site down. I thought that if they shut it down I would lose my job, and I didn't want to lose my job. It was the first real job I had ever had. In fact, I wasn't going to lose my job. Nobody lost their job then. We were still a year away from the point where everybody lost their jobs all at once and billion dollar companies became penny stocks and office buildings became empty glass houses next to highways, with nothing of value left except the copper wiring.

I met someone who optimized Web sites for search engines and asked him to help me. He registered Catalogs2Go so it came up first whenever someone went looking for "free stuff." Soon the site was getting two thousand unique users a day and in 1999 you didn't shut down a Web site with that much traffic. The company had a second round of funding and was hiring everyone available, but the e-commerce platform the company was based on didn't work, or didn't work well enough, and we were losing money on every client. I suggested we sell "search engine optimization." I decided we should charge $3,000 a month.

This is the period of my life that makes the least sense. I had my own apartment. I was making more money than I could possibly spend. I was engaged with my work though I recognized its basic absurdity. I was happy, probably as happy as I have ever been. When I tell people my story I talk about group homes, writing, sexual awakening. I talk about rooftops and drugs and relationships. I mention getting clean and graduating high school in two years and going to college only to finish university and fall right back in. I talk about the semester I took off to work as a barker for a live sex show in Amsterdam, and the affair I had with Miriam, the Surinamese cabaret dancer whose husband was in jail for committing some violent crime. But I rarely talk about the fourteen months I spent working for a living in the place where I made most of the friends I'm closest with today, the people I hired. I rarely talk about it even though it's the moment when modern events finally intersected directly with my life and I became part of the world.

I couldn't get permission from my superiors to sell my product, but they weren't saying no. Within six months my little department was billing something like a million dollars. I was given a bonus. I had five full-time employees and my own temps. We hired the search engine expert. He had business cards printed with the job title "Jedi" and sent company-wide emails on the virtues of gambling and getting high and was quickly fired, but it didn't matter. I would promise rankings and then I would tell someone else to figure out how to get them. I was quoted as a search engine expert in the *New York Times*. I didn't even know how it was done. In retrospect I guess it was a consulting model, but everyone wanted to believe we had created some magic software. Because once you admitted that it was just a college grad scratching his head and resubmitting a Web site with different taglines, then you had nothing to sell. The other companies had their own college grads making coffee and working for options.

Late in 1999 and early in 2000, companies were going public very quickly and that was the only point. When I started at the company there were maybe fifteen employees; eight months later there were two hundred. The company, and the industry, was sinking under its own weight. The board brought in a new leadership team and when they arrived they saw that the only thing turning a profit was me and my little crew in the back.

The new players were tan and fat. They organized sales meetings in Vegas with cabanas near the pool and had hookers sent to their rooms on company credit cards. I was given a new title, director of emerging technologies, along with a saleswoman to help me push more search engine optimization. When we talked she put her hand on my thigh, or ran her fingers along my neck, or pressed my ankle with the toe of her shoe. She couldn't sell anything. She didn't seem to know what a search engine was. When someone would try to explain it to her she would gently pull the hem of her skirt over her knees.

And then I was bored with all of it. I closed my office door every day until noon while I wrote my third novel, *What It Means to Love You,* based on Nancy and Pierce, a couple I'd met when I was stripping in Chicago. The real Nancy was a runaway working as a high-priced call girl. She regularly made $2,000 a day. Pierce was older, effortlessly good looking, with a square jaw, long braided hair, and teardrops tattooed beneath his right eye. Nancy wouldn't share her money so Pierce supplemented his income sucking cock in video booths off Halsted Street.

The last time I saw Nancy she gave me a stolen dress, which I returned to Marshall Field's for a $600 credit. The last time I saw Pierce he was throwing bottles from the window of the studio they shared on the tenth floor of an elevator building on Belmont.

"See you later," I said, while the cops stood around him watching him sweep up the glass. But I never did.

Between March 10, 2000, and April 14, 2000, the tech-heavy NASDAQ exchange plunged 35 percent. Other companies had already cleared out. Giant buildings south of the city sat deserted, as if no one had ever been there. Downtown was quiet, even in the middle of the day.

At work things were tense. Someone erased all the emails and documents from my computer. I led a weekly meeting but people stopped showing up. My salesgirl refused to talk to me. I was called in to discuss possible sexual harassment charges.

"What are you talking about?" I asked.

"You've never worked in a corporate environment before. It's normal that you wouldn't understand certain protocols. We'll pay for you to take a class."

Someone warned me, "I don't know what you did . . ."

One weekend I broke into the COO's email. There was a letter from my salesgirl. She wanted to meet him later and get a drink. Then she wanted to do that thing he liked. She also wanted to know when he was going to get rid of me. She was tired of me looking over her shoulder. He urged her to use the other account he'd set up, and yes, he couldn't wait to fuck her, and no, she shouldn't worry about me. He was going to take care of that. Everything was working fine.

The COO and the salesgirl were living together. Her résumé was fake. They'd met in a strip club. He'd left his wife and she'd left her husband. Now the plan was to push me out and take over my product. Although there wasn't any product. The situation was like some cheap spy novel. I've never bothered to write about it because the characters are so black and white. The things they wanted had no lasting value. They weren't conflicted enough to be frauds like most people; they were just liars.

It was a technology company but he had never changed his password. Same for his VP of sales and my new salesgirl. It was amazing, actually, how many people had never changed their passwords from the ones originally assigned: the original password was *welcome.* I printed the emails and took them to the human resources officer. Like most of senior management, he was new. The old-timers looking to cash in had cashed out instead and gone into retirement. A handful of companies would survive, led by Google, but the boom was bust.

HR offered me two weeks severance but I said it was going to take me longer than that to recover. The VP of sales called me in to his office and threatened to have me killed. I told my employees to watch my door and make sure it never closed. A meeting was scheduled for six at night in the boardroom on a Friday. I got the next plane to Los Angeles and went into hiding with Hart Fisher, my first publisher, in Granada Hills.

They cut me a check for $30,000 in exchange for my signature and a promise not to tell. I cashed the check. A month later the company sank permanently beneath the waves.

This would have been the time to return to Chicago, but I didn't. When I left my fiancée I'd burned some bridge I hadn't known existed. It was 2000. Ralph Nader was running for president. Hans Reiser was in Russia working on his file system, fulfilling a million-dollar contract with the Department of Defense. His best friend was keeping his wife company in California while he was away.

CHAPTER 6

*August/September/October; Searching for Nina; The
Marin Headlands; Patty Spells It Out; Hunting Sheep
with Uzis; Lissette in a Dust Storm; Party on a Boat;
Members of the Jury You May Now Be Seated*

On August 19, a large search party organizes to look for Nina
Reiser's remains in the hills behind Hans' house. A call goes
through the California Office of Emergency Services. Search and
rescue volunteers sign up from Alameda and Contra Costa coun-
ties. Dog handlers from around the state respond through the
California Rescue Dog Association. By eight in the morning over
120 volunteers gather at a multijurisdictional, protected watershed at the base of Pinehurst Drive, below the entrance to the
Redwood Recreation Area.

There are equipment trailers filled with lights and tables and
generators. There are computers and desks, shade canopies, porta-
potties. There's a rescue truck, a medical van, repelling gear, a
food service unit able to feed up to two hundred. The volunteers
fill out cards listing their skill levels and special tools they might
have. At the minimum they've all completed a five-week training
and certification course. Many are Type Two, which means they
have an additional thirty hours of training. Some are Type One,
trained for mountain rescue, able to carry forty-five-pound packs
three miles in forty-five minutes.

They are hikers and climbers, outdoor types, interested in finding children and campers lost in the wilderness, capable of doing emergency care up to three hours away from medical services. Some are trained to save people stuck against large walls, off belay, in places like Yosemite. Their focus is usually on rescuing the living but on this day they are looking for a body a year after the crime. The bones, if they find any, will be black, and likely scattered by animals.

The volunteers are divided into teams of five or six, including a cadaver dog and handler. Each searcher has a radio and reports to two supervisors stationed at the watershed. Throughout the day, dispatch sends food and supplies. Everyone knows this will likely be the last major search for Nina's body. The searchers are instructed to go one hundred feet from the trails and not take any risks. The fire roads are clear but most of the paths are tight and dusty. Poison oak is everywhere. The trees merge above the trails, blocking the sun. Throughout the area there are steep drops but so much growth it doesn't seem that a body would clear without getting hung in the brush. There are places where, if a body did clear the ridge to the valley floor, it would never be found.

In any murder there are thousands of pieces of evidence but only one body, so the searchers hope to find a clue: a scrap of clothing, a piece of jewelry, something that could narrow the area to a quadrant where a hundred men and women could comb shoulder to shoulder over every inch of dirt. They're also looking for loose soil. Over time the earth tends to show where holes have been dug. If Nina is buried here, a square of loose earth should be visible somewhere.

In most abduction cases the body is dumped near a roadside or off a trail and then covered in available materials within three hours of the crime. Only a small percentage of abductors give up the location of the body, even after they've been convicted. But usually the body appears on its own: a jogger notices something, a hiker spots an unusual pattern, a sailor sees something floating on the surface of a lake.

The supervisors don't get many calls. They wait anxiously. The sun is high and the sky is clear. Almost exactly the same weather as on September 3, 2006, the day Nina disappeared. The searchers cover miles through the hills, grid-searching potential plots when they find them. As the day is about to end, a dog reacts to an area twenty feet off the trail near Skyline gate. One of the supervisors, Frank Moschetti, calls the team back and sends another dog into the space without telling the handler they may have found something. The second dog has a milder reaction. Moschetti sends a third dog. That dog reacts strongly. Moschetti calls in a crew of metal detectors and they scan the ground, figuring Nina was probably wearing a ring when she was buried, but the metal detectors don't catch anything. As the sun heads down they start turning over the dirt. They dig slowly, treating the area like an archaeological site. They get three inches below the surface when they hit hardpack. Untouched. Solid earth.

"It's a year after the fact and dogs can be wrong," Moschetti says. "They're just like people that way. Our odds of finding her after this much time has passed, based on the terrain and the number of searchers, was at most around 2 percent. Still, you have to look."

Following the search, Hans' trial is delayed to the beginning of November. It's like waiting for Godot.

From the headlands north of San Francisco the ocean appears calm. Tankers sit like ducks on the Pacific, motoring slowly toward the Golden Gate. There used to be armaments studding these hilltops, waiting for a Japanese attack that never came; now the cannons and big guns are just bronze memorials. It's dusk and there are few people on the hiking trail. The woods in the Oakland hills are dense, rocky, and unwelcoming. The Marin headlands are bright and open, as if they were created with a postcard in mind.

"It's so romantic," Katie says, leaning in for another kiss. I run my fingers through her red hair, which falls past her shoulders in long curls. Katie is also a writer with a book of stories coming out, but she makes her living spinning advertising copy downtown.

"I really like Josie," Katie says, as we continue our walk. She's been reading draft pages from this book. She went through it quickly, looking to see where I mentioned other women, then read it more slowly.

"I thought you would."

Katie's from South Carolina and, like Josie, grew up in a world based on manners and debutante balls. They both knew when it was appropriate to eat and how to give a compliment, and spent a lot of time saying hello and goodbye.

Working toward Coyote Peak, she says, "I've been thinking about Hubert Selby Jr. About writing about people you hate from a place of love. Have you considered forgiving your father?"

A jogger passes us. A woman running alone.

"I don't hate him," I tell Katie. "It's not the things my father did before, it's the things he does now. He's just a man of extreme moods. I think if I was really injured or sick he'd take care of me. Sometimes he carries jackets in the trunk of his car that he gives to homeless people." I tell Katie I recently got a letter from a woman who has been corresponding with my father. They met on one of the dating sites. He took ten years off his age and told her he was a retired sheriff. The woman said she asked my father about me and he told her his son died in 2004. I asked her why she was telling me this and she said she needed to know the truth. She said it was driving her insane. I blocked her email address. It's not the first note I've received from one of his girlfriends. My father spends all his days emailing and meeting women online. He's spent his life this way, not online but moving from one woman to another. He cheated on my mother every chance he got, which was plenty because he tried hard. He used to meet them through personal ads and kept their pictures on the top shelf in a cabinet. That's where I first saw the woman who would become my stepmother, smiling awkwardly, sitting cross-legged and wearing a blue bikini. I lay on the couch in the basement, holding her picture in one hand. My mother was upstairs dying and I was fantasizing about the woman sleeping with her husband. "She's your mother's best friend," my father said when he started bringing her to the house.

"I don't want you to end up like my father," Katie says. "He's sixty-five years old and he still blames his dad for all his problems."

I nod my head. I don't want to be like her father either, an old man who drinks until he's numb and lays down close to $100,000 to send his daughter to an overpriced writing program so she can figure out what to do with her life. An adult who never grew up and doesn't notice his wife is biding her time, waiting for him to die.

When we finish the hike we drive into Sausalito. Katie tells me about her time in New York. She met a boy there and they were happy for a while. But then one day she broke up with him. She said, "I just don't love you," even though she did. She immediately regretted it and spent two years trying to get him back but he wouldn't talk to her anymore. That's what the twenties are for, those kind of mistakes. The thirties are about making compromises. I like lying in bed with Katie at night, burying my nose in her hair. She lives at the front of a small park and the sounds of the park filter through her windows. I like watching her in the morning, sliding her small, muscular body into a dress. We've been together almost a month now and try not to talk about it, but after a few drinks she says, "I'm just worried that I'm not fulfilling you."

"You don't have to worry about that."

"Well," she says. "I like sex. And we haven't had it."

"That's a bigger problem," I concede.

After dark Katie and I make our way back to the city, which looks like a miniature diorama in the distance, beyond the sailboats bouncing in the docks. Rounding the pier I'm struck by the image of the hill on the edge of Sausalito and all the houses facing the bay. It's almost midnight and there are so many windows lit.

I've been moving things into Katie's. Little things: books, a razor, a clean shirt. We cook meals together and watch DVDs. We watch *Stardust Memories,* the train full of gorgeous people having a good time pulling out of the station, leaving Woody Allen behind. We watch season two of *The Sopranos,* Tony telling his doctor, "I don't need therapy; I have life."

I'm sitting in her large chair with my feet up. It's a thick, comfortable chair. I'm working on this book, which is supposed to be about a murder, but I'm not sure where I'm going with it. To write about oneself honestly one has to admit a certain inconsistency and randomness that would never be tolerated in even the best of novels.

Katie sprawls across me, crying. She's been seeing someone else since a little before we met. She likes him and she likes me too.

"Last night," she says. "I was going to break up with you. But I was enjoying your company too much."

I keep my arms around her. I feel my stomach harden and try to look behind us into that little room where she keeps her washer/dryer. I was with her when she picked that thing up. We'd gone to the Best Buy below the highway. The store was full of bright plastics, shelves covered in gadgets nobody needed. We found help from a salesman in a blue polo. *This is what couples do,* I thought. We debated the merits of upright and top-load washers, taking into account space and energy savings. We asked when the delivery would arrive. It was reassuringly mundane. There would be no more girls in the park. No porn stars. No meeting women in Michigan hotel rooms who would burn me with their cigarettes. That time of my life was over.

Beyond the laundry room is the yard with its bright garden and then the green backside of Bernal Heights rising half a mile into the sky, dogs running laps around its peak, their owners looking casually across the city to the bridge. And still, down on earth, I am on Katie's red chair and she is crying in my shirt.

The other day I saw Patty, an old girlfriend of mine. Actually, the first person I ever tried to have a serious sadomasochistic relationship with. It was her birthday and we had decided to get a drink together. She's ten years older than I am and owns a high-end jewelry store in North Beach. When we first met she asked if I was OK with taller women and I told her I was. That was six years ago and we were both looking for something other than sex.

On the way to the bar I told her about Katie. I said maybe I was falling in love. I said I was surprised by how comfortable I felt. I hadn't even realized this was what I wanted. Patty responded with a story about an acquaintance of hers. He's fifty years old and good looking for his age, with a good job near a university in Arkansas. But he's a masochist, driven heavily by his desires, and recently he had been trying to make peace with the idea that he would probably never have an actual partner. He would spend his life alone. We were outside of a supermarket when Patty told me the story and I said I would just go inside and grab a sandwich and meet her in the bar across the street. I found my way to the deli aisle and burst into tears.

I run my finger along Katie's cheek. I tell Katie I'm not trying to audition to be her boyfriend. She'll have to make up her own mind and fuck whoever she wants.

"This is not a phase for me," Katie says. "I don't want to be a character in your stories. This is who I am."

"Hey," I say. "Hey. I've been here the whole time."

For a moment I thought I knew the narrative. But I don't. I never do. I've had too many false starts. I can see it in my own writing, this book functioning as an external memory I go over every day. Miranda doesn't talk to me, Lissette doesn't talk to me, Josie doesn't talk to me. What is Katie, with her clean face and freckles and cute little running clothes doing with me anyway? Or maybe the question is, Why am I with her?

In *The White Album* Joan Didion famously wrote, *"We tell ourselves stories in order to live."* But the point of her essay is that the stories aren't true. I meet with two homicide officers who say Sean sounds like a liar. A forensic psychologist tells me Sean is probably a megalomaniac, trying to reclaim some of the power that was taken from him in his youth. It's the kind of thing these people always say: cause/effect/conclusion. But what about coincidence and fate? Perhaps that's what Didion was trying to get at but wasn't willing to say. Perhaps it was dawning on her that we can't assign motives to other people and the knowledge was driving her crazy.

When I met with Sean he said, "Don't worry. You don't have to be afraid of me." The threat was implicit. He would say it with this neat little smile. The smile of someone older and more experienced. Was he reclaiming power or just enjoying the attention? He said the same thing to the other news outlets that interviewed him. "Don't worry. I haven't killed anyone in a *long* time." Sean confessed to killing eight people and the best cops in Oakland traced the lines and decided not to make the arrest. Sean is a puzzle to me. He says he'll tell me everything I want to know after Hans' trial is over. It's like Rex Hoffman in *The Vanishing*. The criminal tells Hoffman that if he wants to know what happened to his wife, he'll have to drink a potion. Hoffman wakes up in a coffin, buried alive.

I'm with Katie on her couch. It's ten or so at night. I brought home a couple of burritos and the tinfoil sits on the empty blue plates. The TV is disconnected in the center of the room. She says, "I don't think this can work."

After Katie breaks up with me I catch a ride to the Burning Man Art Festival six hours outside San Francisco in the Nevada salt flats. The same festival Hans' mother was attending the weekend Nina disappeared. Burning Man lasts for more than a week and the open playa becomes a city of thirty thousand, a giant party filled with powder, pills, music, and disposable art.

"I wasn't going to come back here," I say to an old man from Tel Aviv. We're under a shade canopy, resting our feet in the cold water of a child's pool where people dump the melted ice from their coolers.

"But here you are."

"Here I am."

He asks if I would like some mushrooms but I say no. I tell him the last time I was here was 2001 when I came straight from doing a story in the Middle East, hanging out with kids throwing bottles of gas at Israeli soldiers in Hebron. I spent a month in Jerusalem and the occupied territories at the height of the Second Intifada. I was full of conflict. When I got to Burning Man all the drugs and "I love yous" were too much.

"I was there in the beginning," the old man says. "I graduated high school just after the Six Day War in 1967. I served two years in the military as commander of a ceremonial guard for the central commander, Rehavam Ze'evi, killed many years later in his hotel."

"I remember," I say. "Israel responded by taking over the Palestinian Authority building in East Jerusalem. Then there was the Sbarro's bombing and the next day the flattened police station in Ramallah. Maybe I have the order wrong. I was there for all of that. It was just before 9/11."

"In 1967," he says, "we took Gaza from Egypt, the Golan Heights from Syria, the West Bank from Jordan. My group was slightly renegade, disorganized. We didn't bother anybody and we didn't want to be bothered. Our job was to stand at attention, make Ze'evi look important. But I'll tell you what, he was a fascist. He thrived on hatred. We were a small unit, just two combat jeeps with noncombat soldiers. Then we were put on an interim deployment and sent to the Jordan River where the Palestinians had been told not to graze their sheep because the sheep would cover the tracks of militants crossing the border at night. But sheep don't understand military law and shepherds have habits. When a herd came within the forbidden zone we were to kill two sheep to teach the Palestinians a lesson. This was not some form in triplicate. This is just what we were told.

"For one reason or another we started killing more sheep.

There would be a large herd and we would think that the shepherd would not learn his lesson if we killed only two. Then we were angry with the Palestinians for some reason. And the truth is it became fun; we were all alone near a forbidden border. Killing sheep became a blood sport. We would chase them with uzis.

"That's how it was in the beginning. It was obvious where things were going to go."

I stay five nights in the desert. The day before I leave a gust of cool wind shoots into the playa. The sun has warmed the ground and a wall of dust leaps into the air. I see Lissette in the middle of the storm with a scarf wrapped over her mouth, wearing goggles and corduroy overalls. I only recognize her by the tattoos on her back, thick black vines weaving toward her shoulders. I touch her arm and we stare at each other through the haze before deciding to sit on the ground outside the center camp while the storm builds and we're covered in a thick layer of alkali and sediment. I slide my hand inside her overalls, across her stomach. She tells me about her new boyfriend and her new job at a public relations firm. "I'm training for a marathon," she says. "I only have two hours a day to see friends, between nine and eleven. It works fine because my boyfriend lives a couple of blocks away. I'm taking a few days off for the festival."

I don't mention Katie. Lissette doesn't like to hear about other women. I ask about Sean. She laughs and says a couple months ago we both called her to complain about each other within half an hour. The storm grows so we can see only a few feet in the distance. It's like staring at a sheet of paper. I wonder if this is healthy, all this stuff from the ancient lake working its way into our lungs, and why Lissette didn't tell me earlier about Sean's phone call. I realize that to Lissette, Sean and I are both the same, just a couple of boys calling to complain. Lissette and I spent eighteen months together and somehow avoided really getting to know each other. We once spent four days in bed together. I never even answered the phone. It was magical actually, such perfect concentration. To only want and think of one person. To not respond to email or indulge in any distraction. To be perfectly focused until you memorize every pore and tiny hair on the tip of a person's nose. I planned my entire existence around her, lived off her affection. Whenever we went out my only concern was to get her alone again. It was the purest, most uncomplicated emotion I'd ever felt. I was devoured by longing.

I slide my hand over her hip; it fits perfectly. I stretch my pinkie and brush the top of her pubic hair.

Lissette says Sean has been very nice to many people she knows. He's generous with his money and time. He's someone who can be counted on, almost pathologically loyal. All he wants is loyalty back. Beyond that, he's selfless. I remember Sean inviting me to volunteer with him in the soup kitchen on Sundays. He asked if I did any volunteer work and I mentioned a tutoring center where I occasionally host panels. He said he would be delighted to volunteer with me and invited me to the shelter. Should I write about someone so conscientiously good? I never lied to Sean. I told him he wouldn't like what I wrote and he wouldn't have any editorial approval. And anyway, he's the one claiming to have killed eight people. When I asked him about the family and loved ones of the people he killed he said that wasn't his problem. How could it not be his problem? A small child sleeps at night; a length of wire slips into her father's throat in the other room. A man leans over a waste bin, puking blood in front of his wife. When Sean talked about there being "fewer abusers on the street than before," it was obvious he saw himself as a heroic figure. He probably wakes most days wondering how to make the world a better place. What about Lissette? Am I stealing from her, pillaging our time together for a handful of anecdotes?

"It's nice you guys are still on good terms," I say about Lissette's husband. She's here with him, sharing a camping spot.

"We've known each other since 1991," she replies.

We'd only been together a couple of weeks when I met Lissette's husband. It was important to her that we meet because that was what honesty meant to her. I was surprised by how good looking he was. She said that he was the most important person in her life and I assured her I was comfortable being number two. But if I suggested leaving town for work or something else she would get quiet and not want to see me. Then divorce floated into their conversations and I stood panicked on street corners, terrified she would never arrive.

I could say a few words and she would leave. It would be enough just to mention, "Since you, I've had girlfriends too." But I don't. I don't because of the way her thighs feel. Because even though she's not touching me back, rejecting me several times a minute, we're leaning against each other. And finally, as the wind dies, we cross into the information tent and sit on a dust-filled couch and she lays her legs across my legs. I feel her molding over me and begin to fall asleep when she sees a boy she knows. He's young, handsome, and thin. She kisses me on the lips and is gone.

Toward the end of October I start to cry fairly often. I feel the first rush in my throat and my chest tightens. I cry in a carshare returning from a conference in San Jose and near my apartment or talking on the phone when a friend asks how things are going. I keep myself busy helping with a book about countries we should invade, a commentary on what it means to make the case for war. I read sad novels and do my work and feel like I've lost some kind of battle. Of course, I haven't. Hans Reiser's trial is beginning any day. I'll stop crying soon and I'll be happy for a while and that's just how things will go. It's how they always go.

Except.

I'm living in the Mission District again, sharing a one-bedroom apartment with a twenty-six-year-old hipster. The apartment is close to the cafés I like, and the trains. I wondered at first if I wasn't too old to be living like this but woke one night at 2:00 AM and saw my roommate in the kitchen drinking with his buddies, and I realized this is where I belong.

One night three friends come over. We have a pizza and set up a table with four chairs in the dining room to play bridge. My partner and I win continually, four majors, three no-trump, forty leg. Finesse the queen, lose your losers, double when it's right. When bridge is played well it's an elegant game. You get your cards, count your points, try to communicate in the limited language of the bid, a language without nuance or emotion and not open to interpretation. These are three of my best friends. People I met in San Francisco years ago, when I just got here. They're not writers. They're carpenters and engineers. They own their apartments. They're married to brilliant, capable women, and their marriages are absurdly strong. No one I grew up with in Chicago has marriages like these.

When they leave after three hours I clear the dishes and pull the recycling bin down to the street. I lie in bed with *Stoner,* by John Williams.

What did you expect? he thought again.

A kind of joy came upon him, as if borne in on a summer breeze. He dimly recalled that he had been thinking of failure— as if it mattered. It seemed to him now that such thoughts were mean, unworthy of what his life had been.

After a bit I place the book on the sill and look at the ceiling. I can't go on like this, I think. The thought runs through me like electricity. On like what? It's not like I could go see Josie and Tony in their Carolina subdivision, tell them after all these years I've reconsidered my choices. Ask my ex-fiancée and husband if I can move into their basement, play Nintendo with their child. I don't even know if they have a child, but it's a safe assumption. Josie, who was tall and thin, her pale pregnant belly stretched blue and translucent above her wiry pubic hairs. The child growing quickly. Maybe he's six years old, or three, or one. Maybe he's not playing Nintendo yet. Maybe he's just a wrinkled little alien in diapers. An ugly baby, in the way most babies are, who will grow handsome and broad shouldered like both his parents. They wouldn't welcome me into their home. That wouldn't jibe well with their version of the American dream.

My pillow is soaked. I go down to the street, walk along Valencia. It's late and I don't expect to meet anyone. The lights are still on the tennis and basketball courts in Dolores Park. The homeless sleep beneath the trees near the base of the lawn; dark masses curled quietly under bags and clothes, rusted shopping carts on guard nearby. Four Asian boys are still on the court playing two on two across from the high school. I walk to the top of the park and throw up, heaving over a bench, with a view of the Oakland Bay Bridge.

In the morning I feel better. I write a note on my computer: *be strong.* I make a list of people I could have called. Girls, of course. Women who would let me come over and sleep on their couches when I need to, see me through my little episodes. It's not a long list but it's enough. I leave it by the side of my bed so I'll remember it, just in case.

Sometimes I think of this depression setting its hooks in me as a failure of my file system. I call up files I shouldn't be thinking of. I mislabel documents and store them in a folder I'd rather bury.

Modern file systems don't just catalog data; they move it into the best available space. The information is continually shuffled into equal-sized digital blocks. It's the most human part of a computer. We remember events in our lives in specific order and importance relative to our identity. Hans Reiser wanted a perfectly efficient memory tree with no wasted space. In the world he envisioned, rather than just pulling a file, you would re-arrange information and create new files. It is an utterly optimistic vision, built for limitless potential. Capable of forgetting, or remembering, anything. The computer's memory would be entirely fluid and suitable to any purpose. Instead of just naming the file, you would name everything, and store information in smaller and smaller blocks of unequal size, accessing only what you need to realize your goals. That's why he called his company Namesys. Delete guilt, delete failure. The file system was just the beginning.

I pop more pills, doubling my prescribed dosage. When I started taking Adderall I took five milligrams and it would last all day. Now I take twenty-five milligrams. The speed lets me lock into my own thoughts, build and rebuild my framework for understanding the world.

"You have to be careful about not sleeping," Roger tells me. "You can do permanent damage to your memory." I had sent him what I've been writing, my "murder" book. He wants to create a special code so I can call him in an emergency but I tell him it's not necessary. "Are you really that sad?" he asks. "No," I say. "Not usually. Sometimes. It's hard to write about all the boring times in between, which is what most of life is."

It's Friday. There's a party on a boat, just south of the ballpark where Barry Bonds has finished his glorious drug-addled career. The pitchers were taking drugs too. He wasn't competing against tubby old Babe Ruth. He was competing against the new century, Roger Clemens and the pharmaceutical millennium. He wanted it more than anyone. He didn't worry about the side effects; his home runs sailed past the bleachers, clearing the wall and landing in the tiny inlet that makes up the China Basin below downtown.

The city has built a new train line in this area, from the ball-park to the shipyards. The University of California is expanding and all the empty lots are sectioned off, filled with bulldozers and trailers. The eastern side of the city is the only place left where any kind of development is possible. The city owns the land but we're selling it for as much as we can get. The last of San Francisco's poor will be pulled from the earth like weeds. Where will they go?

The trial starts.

BOOK 2

The Trial

"Then one of those things happened of which night-mares are made of."

—Neil Elliott, *A Love Story and A Mystery,*
unpublished

"'Everything straight lies,' murmured the dwarf disdainfully. 'All truth is crooked, time itself is a circle.'"

—Friedrich Wilhelm Nietzsche,
Thus Spoke Zarathustra

"You're going to be sorry for not loving me."

—Ricardo Zambrano to the woman
he planned to rape and murder

CHAPTER 7

*November; A Murder Trial Begins; Birthday Parties
and Police Stations; The Children's Doctor; Sons and
Mothers; An Angry Phone Call; Cori's Drawing; The
Missing Car Seat; The Point of the Defense*

There's a twenty-one minute video taken in 2005 of a boy's sixth birthday party at a children's gym in Emeryville, a shopping mall-packed landfill wedged between Oakland and Berkeley. It's an ordinary party. A dozen children run races on rubber mats, dive headfirst into foam pools, crawl through tunnels, and flip over horse bars. The soundtrack is filled with screaming and giggling and the instructions of counselors in the background.

Ten minutes in, the camera centers on the mother bouncing on the trampoline with the birthday boy and his younger sister. She's barefoot, wearing a green and white print dress. She doesn't look like a woman with two children, though maybe that's just a stereotype. She's gorgeous and full of energy. She doesn't look like a murder victim and she's nothing like a movie star. Her beauty is warm and lacking in glamour. She's in her thirties, but there's something younger about her. Her focus on the children is so complete it's as if there were no one else in the entire world.

Hours are like weeks at this age, minutes disproportionate to a world children are only starting to notice. These images are all that will last. The dress hugs the woman's hips and floats toward her knees as she falls. The kids jump as high as they can to impress their mother. There are three men who love her. Within a year one of them will kill her. The lens tries to hold her, the viewer rising and dropping imperceptibly, the steady male gaze of the man holding the camera.

At the end of the video all the children sit around a long table. The mother comes from behind her son with a large knife in her hand. She wraps her arm around the boy, holding him against her breast, while she cuts into the cake.

Officer Benson was manning the desk at the Oakland police station when the mother arrived and took a seat in the open vestibule. She came every Wednesday, always early or on time, and Benson looked forward to seeing her.

The husband arrived late with his four-year-old daughter and six-year-old son, playing with the children before surrendering them. Benson thought he was trying to antagonize her, he thought the father stood too close. He'd spent twenty-seven years on the force, enough time to recognize the messages implicit in the way a man holds his shoulders and squeezes his fists, the self-justifying set of a man's mouth. And he could tell when a mother cared about her children and when she didn't. He'd seen it both ways.

The father was not a large man yet he loomed over the wife who ignored him as she zipped the children's jackets and took their hands. It's always like this, the late arrival, the big show, the husband like a kernel of corn shivering on a hot pan as the pretty woman with the soft accent gathers her children together and says goodbye as if nothing is wrong.

But this time something was wrong. Benson abandoned his desk and walked outside. The father crossed the street, opened the door to a small hatchback, and drove away. The lights went on in the minivan as the children climbed inside. The night was clear. The buildings of downtown like dark obelisks framed against the hills in the distance.

The mother waved as she drove off. He nodded then turned back to the station. He was going to give her some advice next time she came in. He was going to tell her in all seriousness, "You better get yourself a gun."

"Remain seated. Court is now in session."

There he is, the husband, the father, Hans Reiser, sitting with his attorneys at a large table in the middle of Alameda County Courtroom Nine. No one would ever notice him walking down the street, but now he's the center of attention. He's small and not quite handsome, with dark curly hair and the beginning of a bald patch blossoming on his crown. His bright lips come to sharp points high on his cheeks, giving him a resemblance to Jack Nicholson's portrayal of the Joker. Two bailiffs sit behind Hans at a small industrial desk, and behind them, after a low wall, are the sixty wooden seats of the gallery.

He's lost a lot of weight in the year since he was accused of killing his wife. Caught on surveillance cameras in the weeks after Nina's disappearance, he was fat with deep rings circling his eyes. He's changed even since I last saw him six months ago during the preliminary hearings wearing yellow prison fatigues, standing in the prisoner pen holding a box full of papers. Now his features are pronounced, as if his face has come into focus. He's probably never looked this good.

The room around him is high and wide with smooth wood panels slicing between slabs of white stone wrapping the walls. Decorated plates separate the top and bottom windows, which offer a view of Lake Merritt. On the left sixteen padded juror chairs sit empty; on the right is a mounted flat monitor for exhibitions of evidence. In front, framed by an American and California flag and a bronze seal of the state, sits Judge Larry J. Goodman, a veteran of capital cases. Compact, with ruddy cheeks, Goodman has a reputation for casualness, late starts, early dismissals, and two-hour lunches. Beneath his robe he wears a T-shirt and jeans. His court hears only three or four cases a year and he knows as well as anyone that if every killer in Alameda demanded a trial, the system would collapse into chaos. "If it's a felony in Sonoma," he's fond of saying, "it's a misdemeanor in Oakland."

Near the witness box stands a portrait of Nina Reiser holding Cori. She smiles at the photographer. The naked child seems huge against her. In the divorce filings Hans accused Nina of having an affair with the photographer. I wait for Hans to look at the picture of his wife and son but he doesn't for a long time, working instead through the great stack of papers in front of him and occasionally arguing with his lawyers. When he does look up, one hour, two hours later, he glances at Nina's picture but nothing happens to his face.

William Du Bois, Hans' lead defense attorney, stands behind Hans massaging his shoulders while they wait. Du Bois' jacket stretches across his broad back. He wears his collar high and tight around his thick neck so he resembles a well-dressed turtle. There have been rumors that Hans will fire Du Bois and defend himself. I watch the attorney's fingers, burrowing into the navy coat, the fabric gathering at his fingertips.

In the hallway the reporters ask about the arguments Du Bois has been having with his client. "It's hard defending someone so smart," Du Bois says. "He can memorize nine thousand pages of discovery so sometimes he catches mistakes in testimony and he gets upset." Then he adds, as if surprised he'd just thought of it, "You'd be upset too if you were falsely accused of murdering your wife."

The court is packed for opening statements. There are a dozen journalists and people who live nearby and have nothing better to do. There are police officers with an interest and a woman who served on a jury that District Attorney Paul Hora argued in front of before. It was his most famous case, the trial of Stuart Alexander, the Sausage King. Stuart was caught on his own security cameras executing three meat inspectors at his San Leandro plant, returning to shoot each in the head. That trial lasted seven and a half months and the killer was sentenced to death.[11]

"He's a wonderful man," the ex-juror says.

Hora is over six feet tall, trim and rigidly straight. He says he's going to introduce us to someone who's not going to testify at the trial. "She was a mother," he tells the jury, pointing at the picture. "And she would never, *ever,* have abandoned those kids." He shows pictures from the inside of her house. On the refrigerator are photographs of the children above a whiteboard detailing their lunch menu for the next seven days.

"In 2004, after five years," Hora explains, "she left Hans for his

---

11. Stuart Alexander died in prison a year later.

best friend, Sean Sturgeon. She shouldn't have done it. Nonetheless it happens." In late 2005 Nina left Sean for Anthony Zografos.

When it's Du Bois' turn, he takes his glasses off and pulls on the bridge of his nose. "Here we have something," he says, squinting his eyes, showing an image from a black and white magazine advertising Eastern European women. Nina smiles above an ad for Nina5972, a university student looking for a serious relationship. *You see,* he seems to be saying. *What kind of woman has her picture in a magazine like this? A mysterious woman, that's who. The kind that disappears.*

Du Bois refers to the men who had keys to Nina's apartment as "the key club" but he only names Anthony and Sean as members. He shows a picture of Nina and Sean. "An interesting character, Sean Sturgeon. A drug addict. A sadomasochist."

Du Bois portrays Nina as promiscuous, but offers little to back it up. He says she kept pictures of the children around because she was concerned about her own image. She wanted people to believe she was a good mother, which is not the same as being one. It quickly seems like Nina's the one on trial, but she's not here to defend herself.

During recess one of the local newscasters says to me, "They're never going to convict him. That girl was a freak." The newscaster is well known, at least on this side of the bridge, and dresses in tailored beige suits for his reports on the morning news. He's built like a quarterback, with a square, rugged face. I imagine doing a little research, finding out what he's into, how many times he's cheated on his wife, and posting pictures with his statistics. It wouldn't take much.

I wake before court at six and pop my pill before typing my notes. I like going to court every day. I like the structure. A parade of schoolteachers take the stand. They recall Nina volunteering, escorting the children on field trips, bringing home and washing the class towels. Ron Zeno, the executive director of Safe Exchange, says every time Nina walked through the door she would get down on one knee, spread her hands, and the children would rush into her arms. Hans told Ron, "You'd be surprised if you knew what she was into. If you knew what her boyfriend was into."

According to witnesses Hans, the opposite of Nina, was openly hostile toward them. A parent from the school remembers a party during which Hans stated that his family was a burden to him and that he'd be better off financially if he didn't have to take care of them. An instructor recalls Hans interrupting her class to force Cori to write cursive for an hour, and the principal recalls having to talk to Hans about his disruptive behavior. He was irresponsible with the kids' documents, always late, incapable of even cleaning up after himself. He treated his mother like a servant. Some Monday mornings, after his weekend with the children, Hans' mother would have to call Nina and ask if she could come help get the children to school.

Paul LaRosa from *48 Hours* tells me Hans is the least sympathetic defendant he's ever seen.

After Nina left Hans, he sent her notes, one of which said, *"I think you are evil because you cannot help it."* He made threats, like *"Those that are slow to anger are slow to cool."* He became defined by a hatred of his wife so pure and radiant it obliterated everything in its path. *"It is June 1941,"* he wrote, *"and you are the Nazis and you think we will not suffer the necessary amount to defeat you. We will."*

When Hans met Nina he was like all clients of bride services: he was searching for a good deal, a woman who was smarter, prettier, and kinder than the women willing to spend time with him back home. He paid $20 for Nina's contact information. He didn't think that maybe she was looking for something too. Nina had her own ambitions. Hans told Nina he was a famous scientist, and he might have been. The only thing holding back wider acceptance of his innovations was his personality. He thought if he brought Nina to America she would be so grateful she would love him forever, ignore his narcissism, his months away, his bitter ugly view of the world. Hans thought he could convince her to love him without becoming loveable. He was wrong about that. No relationship can survive contempt. Every con is based on the mark's own greed.

"You're transferring," my friend Kay says. "You think Nina is your mother and Hans is your father." Several times a week I call Kay to talk about the trial. Because her mother is a psychologist she often sees the world through subconscious motivations.

"That's ridiculous," I say. But I do find myself pulled toward Nina, understanding the fierce attractions in orbit around her. Who doesn't want a mother who volunteers at the school, won't accept a job that won't give her time with her children, and keeps a dry erase board with a meal schedule on the fridge so you always know what to expect?

Hans was convinced that Nina had Munchausen syndrome by proxy, a rare disorder in which the affected create illnesses for their children to draw attention to themselves. He reported her to the child abuse hotline, explaining for over half an hour how his estranged wife was forcing their son into unnecessary medical procedures because she wanted the boy to be weak, because she hated him. The decision was made not to investigate.

The children's doctor remembers Cori, three years old, throwing a tantrum, and Nina on her hands and knees, whispering to him until he calmed down. The pediatrician ended treatment after receiving a threatening phone call from Hans. Cori was suffering hearing loss and sharp pains and needed his adenoids removed, a routine procedure similar to removing tonsils. Hans said he would sue the doctor if she went forward with the operation. He had been reading up on the subject. The problem, he thought, was probably allergies related to Nina's cat.

I close my eyes when the doctor recounts the call. I have a collection of correspondence between the local hospital and my father. My mother is dying of multiple sclerosis and they're refusing to offer treatment. In his letters to Swedish Covenant, he wrote it was too much of a burden to drive his sick wife to another hospital farther away, but they wouldn't relent. He was too disruptive, too threatening. When he sent me the letters along with his clippings and his unpublished memoir he must have thought I would see his side of the story. He kept the letters twenty years, evidence of the wrong done to him. But I know exactly why that hospital refused treatment to my mother. My father strongly distrusted doctors. Like Hans, he thought people were stupid, especially experts. What was the point of a college degree when it was so easy to lie on a résumé? My father was fond of books full of predictions made by specialists who turned out to be false. He was accustomed to people backing down and wasn't aware of the effect his temper had on others. In his memoir he writes about my mother's friends failing her, not coming around to keep her company after she fell ill. He doesn't remember slamming the door so hard it seemed the frames would splinter, and screaming, "Get the fuck out of my house!"

"I'll leave him," my mother told me once, struggling to hold her chin high. "I'll get better and I'll go back to England. You'll see." I was ten or eleven years old, sitting on the couch with her, the end of her blanket across my knees. We'd turned the television off and the house was stunned silent. I don't know if my father had just gone into the bedroom, or his basement office, or left again to meet one of his other women somewhere in the city. But there had been yelling, the kind you never get used to. It came from nowhere, or a place I was too young to understand. The noise was so loud, the violence crashing toward us until our ears threatened to pop. There was name calling; I was a cocksucker, motherfucker. There were accusations: "When we got married we had a bargain. I make the money and you take care

of the children. You're not living up to your end of the bargain."
We sat in the hum that always followed, a silence you could feel
creeping across your skin like gel.

I was just starting to use drugs, opening the window near my
bed at night, dropping softly onto the lawn. Running with Roger,
Javier, and Justin to the park two blocks away. My mother was
crying and angry, exhausted, trying and failing to keep her head
steady, to sit forward. She wanted me to believe she could stand
up for herself. But she couldn't. And I couldn't stand up for her.
Or I could have, but I didn't. She should have gone, the day of her
diagnosis, home to her parents and sisters in the small hill town
outside of Sheffield, England. But it was too late now. Instead she
was stuck in the North Side of Chicago. Her body became her
prison. Her head shook violently and she leaned back against the
pillow.[12]

As I got older and my mother got sicker she stopped confid-
ing in me. I avoided her, or badgered her for money, with the result that my father stopped leaving money with her. She didn't
complain anymore when she smelled cigarette smoke on my
clothes or notice the streaks on my face that were left from inhaling spraypaint out of a plastic bag halfway down the alley. A
year before she died, recognizing something in my look, she told
me if I ran away, it would kill her. I didn't want the responsibility
so I waited. I came home as little as possible, just long enough to
do my chores: empty the bucket of urine next to the couch, wash
the dishes, take out the trash, maybe make her a cup of instant
coffee with lots of milk, maybe open myself a can of something
to eat. Like her friends, I was chased away by my father's rage.
Transformed by it, perhaps. That's what the caseworkers could

---

12. My mother's type of MS is much less common today following the
advent of drug treatments in the mid-nineties.

never understand. It wasn't the handcuffs or the beatings or his shaving my head. That was nothing. It was the terror. I stayed away. I grew my hair out, skipped school, wore tattered rock T-shirts held together with safety pins. While the chemo glowed across my mother's atrophied frame I sat in the metal pumpkin at Indian Boundary Park, slid another hit of sunshine below my tongue, and waited for the gang to arrive. My mother cried frequently and I have a distinct impression toward the end she didn't care for me too much. I hadn't given her reason to. If she had gone into remission she might have left me behind as well. People tell me it's not true but I don't see how they would know.

Hans' mother, Beverly Palmer, wears a cobalt blue skirt that runs to her ankles and a matching jacket with a neck collar. She's almost seventy years old, with defenseless, wide-open eyes. Her bright copper hair, streaked with gold and white, rises in dry curls like an electric storm.

She takes the stand for two days but can hardly remember anything. She remembers Hans telling her he was sleeping in his car in the period between when Nina went missing and when he was arrested and charged with murder five weeks later. She wants to believe her only child isn't a killer and that Nina is hiding somewhere. She doesn't recall saying Nina was extremely conscientious and that leaving the children would be atypical of her, totally out of character, but she doesn't dispute it's her voice on the recording. She remembers being concerned about Nina's disappearance but she doesn't remember telling the police Nina was a lovely person. "I think people are a mixture of things."

When Palmer came back from Nevada Tuesday night, September 5, Hans met her at her friend's house. They were unpacking their things after a trip to the Burning Man Festival. Hans got a call while he was waiting. It was Nina's friend Ellen and a police officer. "Nina has been missing for two days," Ellen said. "You were the last to see her. Do you know where she might be?"

"You'll have to talk to my lawyer about that," Hans said, and hung up the phone.

When his mother was ready to go it was almost ten o'clock. Hans said he had something to tell her but it would upset her so he would tell her in the morning. She thought he wanted to borrow money again. He already owed her $40,000. But what he wanted to tell her was that the mother of her grandchildren was gone.

The next day Palmer found out that Hans had bought all new towels and stolen her car. She has two cars, a Honda Hybrid and a CRX that Hans often used. He wouldn't give her back the Hybrid. She asked where the CRX was and he wouldn't say. Up in the hills, without a car, you're stranded. Hora asks why she didn't call the police.

"I'm his mother," she says.

"So if he wants he can just take both cars?" Hora asks.

"I guess that's what it comes to, doesn't it?" she replies. She rented a car instead.

Everything that happened then is just a blur, or she's covering for her son. She remembers the new towels, but can't remember if the old towels were gone. She says the beam in the middle of the living room, where police found a smear of Nina's blood, hadn't been cleaned in twenty years. "I kept meaning to refinish it," she says. "But I never did." When the police found the smear, eleven days after Nina disappeared, the blood was still a bright red. The iron in the blood hadn't rusted into brown like all blood does eventually, and there was no dust or debris on top of the stain.[13]

Under cross-examination, Du Bois asks about her husband, the man she married after leaving Hans' father, who died seven years ago. "Is it fair to say he was the love of your life?"

"He was," she agrees.

"And since he died you have a hard time remembering things. Maybe you no longer care to remember things?"

"That's true. But I've never had a very good memory to begin with."

"Were you taking medication at the time?"

"No."

"Are you taking medication now?"

"Yes."

Hora plays a tape of a call from Hans after the police had tapped Beverly's phone, made September 23, at 9:06 PM:

HANS: *I had wanted to go to a mediator. I guess Nina decided that wouldn't be enough fun. It was more than that. She really had Munchausen by proxy disorder. She came up with these illnesses*

---

13. Blood cannot be dated through DNA testing.

for Cori because she hated me and he was her proxy for me so by discovering he was borderline autistic that was her way of degrading me . . . Cori said he wanted to live only with me. That's because he understands his mother wants him to be sick and doesn't really like him on some deep conflicted level . . . She stole money. And you know, at the time I was asking people to take pay cuts she was spending money like crazy . . . She did things like kick me and then call the police . . . Being decent is a mistake. A mistake I paid for heavily . . . She didn't just abuse me, she looked for every possible way she could screw me and did it. The fact that I'd been a good husband just seemed like weakness to her.

PALMER: *As awful as these things are, it's still sad whatever happened to Nina. Don't you think?*

HANS: *I think my children shouldn't be endangered by her. All I ever wanted was to be nice to her and give her an opportunity to come to the United States.*

PALMER: *But she didn't deserve what happened to her.*

HANS: *Yeah, and neither did I. Neither did my son. The whole court system made it so much worse than it had to be. These lawyers systematically drained us of everything we had . . . It may be hard to reach me for a while . . . Bye mom. I love you a lot.*

BEVERLY: *Ha. Good. Bye bye.*

"You remember that call?"

"Yes. Vaguely."

"Why did you sound so surprised at the end when he said he loved you?"

"I was nervous."

"You were nervous?"

"How could one not be nervous about this?"

"You mean when he calls you up and tells you how much he hates Nina twenty days after she disappeared. That made you nervous?"

On September 18, 2006, two weeks after Nina disappeared, Hans met Artem Mishim at a custody hearing for Hans' children. The county had taken the children. Hans knew Artem from the judo academy where he took classes and Artem had agreed to be a character witness.

"How's it going, Scott?" Artem said. He was making a joke, referring to Scott Peterson. After court they left together, driving a strange path through Berkeley, avoiding the highway and major streets, then stopping for dinner on Solano Avenue. Following dinner they looked beneath the car, as if they were worried someone had placed a tracking device. At the end of the evening Artem dropped Hans in Berkeley and Hans walked four blocks to the Honda CRX, which he'd left hidden on a side street. It took him thirty minutes to walk to the car, even though it was five minutes away. He walked around the block, past the car, then doubled back before climbing inside. He drove to the bottom of Shepherd's Canyon, parked the car near the highway where his mother or the police were unlikely to find it, and sprinted up the hill toward his home.

The police had been following Hans the entire day, using at least a dozen vehicles and a fixed-wing plane with glass sides and gyroscope-mounted binoculars. They wanted the CRX, which they thought held the key to unlocking the mystery behind Nina's disappearance. But the car posed more questions than it answered. The CRX had been thoroughly scrubbed, the floors soaked, the compartments holding an inch of standing water. The passenger seat was missing along with whatever it did or didn't contain. Hans was hiding something, but they were moving farther away from finding it.

"Where did he put the seat?" I ask Du Bois during recess.

"He threw it in a dumpster," Du Bois says.

"That doesn't make any sense," I say. "It's one thing to remove a seat, it's another to throw it away. It wasn't even his car."

I ask him about a drawing Cori drew of his father coming down the stairs to the basement where the two children are sleeping, carrying Nina in his arms.

"That's ridiculous," Du Bois says. "Why would Hans carry his dead wife into his children's room?"

"You want us to accept that he's rational when it comes to carrying his dead wife down the stairs, but irrational when he throws away a perfectly good car seat?"

Du Bois barely acknowledges my comment. "All of that will come out in the trial." This is a hallmark of the case, Du Bois promising some exciting new detail in the coming days that will prove his client's innocence, and then failing to deliver. A TV producer asks Judge Goodman if the case is likely to stretch into a fourth month and he says no. "I don't think the defense has much of a case." He means the defense isn't going to call many witnesses, but the subtext is obvious.

I ask Du Bois why the children haven't seen or heard from their mother. "If she wants to carry this charade out she has to stay away from her children for now." It occurs to me that Du Bois must know what he's saying isn't true. Nina's dead and he's aware of that. She's certainly not in Russia, where her disappearance is front-page news. Why would she work so hard to get American citizenship only to frame Hans with a murder, abandon her children, and go into permanent hiding? She wouldn't even know Hans was going to be charged with murder. I point this out to some friends. "He's lying," I say. "He's just doing his job," they reply. Du Bois continues to say everything will be explained in the trial, but I doubt it. I can see how he communicates. The strategy of the defense is to confuse situations. He's not going to answer questions; he's going to propose possibilities. The point is not truth. The point of the defense is that there is no truth.

CHAPTER 8

December/January/February; Sluts, Media Whores, Murderers; Juno; Elizabeth Wurtzel; Proposition 21; Eurasian Goddess; Adolescent Forgiveness; Winter Holidays; Suicide Note or Press Release; Sylvia Plath; Simone Weil; Issues with Women

From the fifth floor of the courthouse I can see the birds gilding the cold surface of Lake Merrit, hiding in the trees on the lawn at the water's edge. The docks are empty, a steady stream of traffic moves like animation on the freeway nearby, the sun paints the west face of a white tenement on the farther shore.

I never meant to write about a murder. It was just a chance comment when I was grasping for anything. "Your guy just confessed to eight murders." I believed it. I wanted it to be true.

In the opening months of the trial my depression lifts. I can see it, like a cloud cresting a mountain range, but I try to pretend it's not there. I read an essay on William Styron by his daughter, now a novelist herself.[14] He had already written *Darkness Visible*, about his first bout of depression that led to eventual hospitalization. It's a profound work on the subject, eighty pages of

---

14. *New Yorker*, December 10, 2007.

straightforward prose, as specific and purposeful as a life vest. It became a number one best seller. Following the publication he toured as an advocate and spokesman for the afflicted, but he never wrote the sequel. His daughter tells of when his depression returned. The second time nothing worked. He was in and out of institutions for fifteen years, incoherent with pills and treatment. He stopped trying to write, as if the author of *Sophie's Choice* was entirely separate from the man in bed on the second floor, refusing to move. He met his wife when he was still that young and brilliant writer. He told her to leave him, but she wouldn't, even though he wasn't a particularly good husband. She entered a new phase of life as his caretaker.

The prosecution is still calling witnesses. Hans' neighbor saw Hans two days after Nina disappeared. It was eleven at night and Hans had just brought his mother home. It was two hours after he was told Nina was missing. It was a sweltering night and the neighbor was on his deck barefoot, in shorts and a T-shirt, watering the rose bushes. He saw Hans in jogging pants and a heavy jacket, dressed for winter, hosing down a section of his driveway for half an hour. What's he doing? the neighbor thought. "He was exhibiting strange behavior, even for Hans."

We also hear from Arthur Gomez, who was in jail with Hans after he'd been arrested when a report came on that a body had been found in the Oakland woods. Hans rushed to the TV.

"That's when I knew he did it," Gomez says.

"And why did you decide to testify?" Du Bois asks.

"I've done some bad things. But killing your wife, that's evil."

"I see. And you would say it's evil to kill your wife but not to smack her around?" he asks, referring to Gomez's second felony conviction. Gomez cracks a smile.

"She wasn't my wife."

We also hear from the investigator who found Nina's van

parked near the highway three miles from Hans' mother's house, her groceries strewn about, an exploded melon in the backseat.

In his office Du Bois has articles mentioning this trial framed on his walls, hung before the trial even started, before he knew if he had won or lost.

I remember Sean telling me, "I can see you enjoy the limelight." He was right. He kept insisting he was the opposite, that he had never looked for attention. But of course he had; he just didn't know it. While he was talking to me he was talking to *20/20*, *48 Hours*, *Wired*. He thinks he knows why he was talking to these people. We all like to think we know why we do what we do. I hear the defense's introduction of Sean as "a drug addict. A *sadomasochist*." Sean said he wouldn't talk to me until after the trial, but at that point he would help with my book. His eight phantom murders hover wraithlike and faceless in the courtroom. Sean won't be testifying. Hora won't call him, and the judge's ruling that Du Bois can't intimate Sean's involvement in the crime renders it pointless for him to call Sean as a witness for the defense.

According to Jung, a stranger can see in an instant something in you that you might spend years learning about yourself. Du Bois harps on the flaws of every witness. How awful we all are when we look at ourselves under a light, finally seeing our reflections. How little we know about ourselves. How much forgiveness it must take to love a person, to choose not to see their flaws, or to see those flaws and love the person anyway. If you never forgive you'll always be alone.

During breaks Du Bois tells us Nina wasn't such a good mother, she was just cultivating an image. He accuses the prosecutor of bringing the case to trial because of the media coverage. But Paul Hora might be the only decent man in the courtroom. Simple and honest, he refers to himself as a Boy Scout, believes deeply in the law, and goes to sleep early at night. He's one of the best prosecutors in the state. He won't talk to the media. His only fault is a tendency to assume guilt in the accused. A small blemish compared to the rest of us: sluts, media whores, murderers.

Elizabeth Wurtzel just turned forty. She's in law school now. Gorgeous, Ivy League educated, a Generation X darling, she was twenty-four when *Prozac Nation* was released. By her second book she was supplementing antidepressants with Ritalin, chopping her pills and snorting them, which led to her third book, *More, Now, Again,* about her addiction to ADD medication. The book was panned by the critics. *Prozac Nation* offered hope for people with depression; they weren't alone with their bottle of pills. *More, Now, Again* destroyed that premise. It turned out the pills didn't work after all. Like *Prozac Nation,* it also ended on a hopeful note, but people no longer believed it. She had shattered her own myth. I wonder if she's given up writing because it was destroying her, or decided that the return on investment doesn't equal the time served. Perhaps the writing was just a symptom of some other insatiable desire. Maybe she'll write an essay here and there but her life is now about other things.

I wonder if I'll have to quit Adderall soon. I keep upping my dosage with diminishing effects. I'm tense all the time. Sometimes I feel so angry I can't recognize myself. I get headaches. The days fuse together and my memory fails me often. At a birthday party on the weekend, I describe *Juno,* which I had seen earlier, to a friend. I loved the movie. It felt familiar, perhaps because it was written by a former stripper, but more because of the average middle-class existence of the children portrayed in the film. They played records and ran track and called each other on hamburger shaped phones. The parents weren't educated or rich but they were decent. It was a world I knew through a looking glass.

The high school in the film existed within my high school, but I didn't go there. "Who'd you see the movie with?" my friend asks. I stare at her for a minute, unsure if I'll be able to recall. "You don't remember?" And then I do, the memory spreading like an ink stain. I make some joke to cover up. We all forget things. I had just seen the movie three hours earlier.

The online message boards are filled with Adderall and Ritalin junkies, popping up to ninety milligrams every day just to get back to where they were before they started. Like every drug it's never as good as the first time. But the alternative seems so much worse. I don't see how I can write anything without the speed. What would I do if I stopped writing? How would I make money? Who would know I was alive? I lie down at night and cover my eyes, eager for the morning pill. When the Adderall works I lose myself. The amphetamine gives me confidence. I forget that no one depends on me in any way. And then one morning I take the framed picture of a juvenile inmate and lay it on my desk. There's the face of the boy in black and white superimposed on a maximum security cell with its door open to reveal the end of a bed. I'd put together a fundraiser for the child years ago. We packed hundreds of people into an art space and showed a film, then listened to activists and spoken word poets. He had been tried as an adult following the passage of Proposition 21, the Pete Wilson bill. Wilson was the governor of California, a man deformed by the force of his own ambition, and the misnamed *Gang Violence and Juvenile Crime Prevention Act* was supposed to propel him to the presidency. It didn't. He broke the backs of the people he stepped on and then burned out and faded away. As far as I know the boy staring at me is still behind bars and will be for the rest of his life. I used to think that if I had worked harder, been more organized, I could have stopped Proposition 21. I was wrong. Proposition 21 passed with 60 percent of the vote. I place a pill above his face and crush it with the back of a credit card and snort it with a rolled-up check. I notice the difference immediately. It's just like cocaine.

I get a letter from a student in Michigan. He's seventeen and friends with the son of a woman I met years ago in a restaurant near the interstate. Later I would send her money, when I had any. She walked in wearing a full-length fur coat, which I took from her before lighting her cigarette. She had fresh injections in her lips, breast implants, and Botox. She lived fifty miles from anything resembling a city, took uppers all day while selling video chats and phone calls and subscriptions to her Web site, which featured pictures of her fully clothed, shopping for books. She was European and Asian and looked like Jessica Rabbit if Jessica Rabbit starred in *Venus in Furs*. I didn't think I had ever seen anybody so beautiful in my entire life. I wanted to be roped against her body, dragged behind her as she went about her day. She said she was a hypnotist and could read my mind. We drank beers from tall glasses shaped like boots before going to my hotel room where I lay on the floor and she walked across me in her heels. She kept taking pictures of herself, posing for her camera set on the dresser.

"I don't like giving people pleasure," she said. Then she sat on the sofa and I kneeled in front of her and she slapped me several times. She held her cigarette near my face and I could feel its heat about to burn my eyelids. She laughed loudly. Then she pressed the cigarette into the back of both my hands. "Those are going to blister."

The blisters, just behind my thumb and index finger, were the size of pencil erasers. At the time I was finishing my novel *Happy Baby*. Flying home, rubbing the yellow nubs behind my knuckles, I wrote what had just happened into the opening of the book. I think of her every time I look at the scars.

The boy who wrote to me includes a picture of himself hanging out with two friends in a park with their hoods pulled over their ears sharing a large bottle of Jack Daniels. He wants to know what I think of his writing. He's in high school and writes on his Web page about his friend's hot mom and his own drug use. I wonder if he knows what his friend's hot mom does to strangers in hotel rooms. His prose is jittery and honest. He writes about drugs correctly, from the vantage point of a lover who doesn't know he's going to be let down.

There was a time in my life when drugs made me deliriously happy. I remember an apartment near the school where one of Justin's girlfriends lived. Six of us sat on the couch laughing for hours while Pat, in a loose blue polyester shirt, imitated Jesus Christ, spreading his arms for crucifixion, the cuffs hanging loosely from his wrists. "I forgive you," he said. "Seriously. You're forgiven." Anne told us to be quiet, she was worried about the downstairs neighbors, but we could have cared less. We weren't going anywhere.

"Why aren't you high?" I asked. "If you were high we wouldn't be so loud."

I remember drinking vodka from clear plastic bottles the night I turned fourteen, in a basement I'd broken into with Justin and Javier. We drank until dawn and in the morning we were woken by the police and told to get out and not come back. They didn't ask where we were going next. I remember smoking joints dipped in PCP, and I remember playing dice for T-shirts on the top floor of the group home, and I remember waking up one morning with a giant dagger tattooed on my shoulder. I remember climbing from the group home window and hanging from the fire escape, my feet resting on the rail for balance. If I put any weight on the rail the stair would lower and there would be nothing beneath me. It was winter and a fine layer of snow covered the city. I was two stories above the pavement, sneaking back and forth between rooms, awed as the hospital melted and everything burned bright all the way to the Robert Taylor Homes, the largest housing projects in the world.[15] I remember crawling along the floor searching for a plastic bag the size of a Lemonhead rumored to have disappeared into the carpet. I remember a heavy metal concert on quaaludes and smoking crack from a pressure gauge and feeling for a moment like everything was possible. Drugs didn't make us loveable, they made us capable of love, gave us the ability to forgive, which had eluded us previously. I remember holding a belt in my mouth and pushing the needle into my vein and sliding happily to the floor.

Now I get prescriptions and use drugs for a different reason. I'm more ambitious and I have less control. When Du Bois described Sean as "a drug addict, a *sadomasochist*," he could easily have been describing me.

Court breaks for the winter holidays and I spend my time rereading my notes. I sit with the lights off looking into the airshaft, imagining Hans Reiser and his cruel disregard. On March 13, 2002, back when they were still friends, Hans sent Sean an email saying Nina would not be the only woman in his life. He said he needed at least five more children. He must have meant boys. He never mentions his daughter in any of his letters. The double standard didn't bother him. He said Nina could take care of the children. He thought he was benevolent and entitled. Following the separation in 2004, Cori acted out in school. After weekends with Hans, Cori told his teachers he didn't need to listen to them because they were women and women shouldn't have any rights in this country. Hans' own

---

15. The Robert Taylor Homes were eventually eclipsed by projects in Brazil and elsewhere.

mother testified that her son was selfish. It doesn't make him
a murderer, though. Not until it's all taken together, all of his
actions in the month following the crime. On September 28,
2006, Hans was picked up and a warrant was served on his
body. He was taken to the station for a DNA swab and photographed nude. He carried $9,000 in cash, his passport, and a
three-page single-spaced typed note.

"I'm a well known scientist," he wrote. *"You get to where you
know someone's methodology is wrong."* He addresses the schoolteachers he believed were conspiring against him. *"I've been telling you about Nina and nobody listens. I would like to thank the
school and teachers for teaching me about how the court works . . .
I may be a danger to the world view of some but I am no danger to
my children."*

It was unclear the point of the letter or why it would be one
of the few possessions in the small fanny pack around his waist.
Later he would say it was a press release. To me it resembles a
suicide note. But he didn't go through with it. He was charged

with murder twelve days later and has been held without bail ever since.

On February 11, 1963, at 6:00 AM, Sylvia Plath went to the children's room and left a plate of bread and butter and two glasses of milk. She wrote a note asking whoever found her to call her doctor, and left the doctor's phone number. Then she turned on the gas and put her head in the oven. The au pair, a young girl from Australia, was supposed to start that day. She arrived at nine, right on time, but nobody came to the door. The neighbor should have been awake but his bedroom was just beneath Sylvia's kitchen and the gas had seeped through the floor, knocking him out cold. The au pair went looking for a telephone to call the agency and make sure she had the right address. When the door finally opened at 11 AM, Sylvia's body was still warm.

In the months preceding her suicide Plath read the *Ariel* poems to A. Alvarez. He heard the despair but chose not to react to it. He critiqued the poems on their own terms, the way Sylvia wanted him to, recognizing the fatal brilliance. Even as she read aloud to him:

> *I do not stir,*
> *The frost makes a flower,*
> *The dew makes a star,*
> *The dead bell,*
> *The dead bell,*
>
> *Somebody's done for*

The last time Alvarez saw Sylvia, on Christmas Eve 1962, he wrote, *"She seemed different. Her hair, which she usually wore in a tight, school-mistressy bun, was loose. It hung straight to her waist*

like a tent, giving her pale face and gaunt figure a curiously deso-
late rapt air, like a priestess emptied out by the rites of her cult.
When she walked in front of me down the hall passage and up the
stairs of her apartment her hair gave off a strong smell, sharp as an
animal . . . When I left about eight o'clock to go to my dinner-party,
I knew I had let her down in some final and unforgivable way. And I
knew she knew. I never again saw her alive."[16]

Plath's last collection culminated in a new era in letters, the
merger of the artist with her art. It was the beginning of the sixties, the Boomers were stepping from beneath Eisenhower's
prosperous shadow. Fifteen years after Plath's death, Susan
Sontag wrote of Goethe and his disdain for Kleist, who submitted
his work, *"on the bended knees of his heart."* Sontag cast a harsh
light across her generation's artistic expectations. *"The morbid,*
the hysterical, the sense of the unhealthy, the enormous indulgence
in suffering out of which Kleist's plays' tales were mined—is just
what we value today."[17] That was thirty years ago. Today's artists
are healthier and no special prizes are given for suffering. It's no
wonder Wurtzel went to law school. The books of our time have
little to do with destruction of the self. We expect our bards to
survive, to figure things out. The literature of triumph over ad-
versity spans every age, but where is the rest of it? We're living
in the most medicated era humanity has ever known. The artist
is no longer expected to play chicken with her creation. Doctors
monitor our intake. We live in the age of Goethe on Zoloft.

My left wrist is riddled like a one-way map. I was a homeless
teenager the last time I pressed a straight razor deep into my arm

---

16. A. Alvarez, *The Savage God: A Study of Suicide* (Random House,
1972), 33.

17. Susan Sontag, *Against Interpretation: And Other Essays* (Macmillan,
2001), 55.

and yanked it out, the flesh blooming from the gash like a red and white rose before I fell to my knees, unsure if I wanted to finish the job or just find a warm place to spend the night. Alvarez was convinced Sylvia did not actually want to die. For one thing, she adored her children. For another, there was the note asking whoever found her to call the doctor and providing the number. Everything was set up for her rescue, but everything went wrong and she died. It's unlikely that if Alvarez was more supportive he could have saved Plath, but we'll never know. She wanted her poetry to be understood on its own terms, even as she ate through herself. Alvarez's description of their last meeting is shockingly cruel, especially given his own history with suicide, which he wrote in a brief epilogue: *"The youth who swallowed the sleeping pills and the man who survived are so utterly different that someone or something must have died."* It's also accurate. The death smell released by the chronically depressed is powerful and repellent. The natural inclination is to recoil. To function one has to hide one's intent. Even when we write about it we keep it to ourselves.

Geoff Dyer came through his depression by following a fascination with D. H. Lawrence. *"One way or another we all have to write our studies of D. H. Lawrence. Even if they will never be published, even if we will never complete them, even if all we are left with after years and years of effort is an unfinished, unfinishable record of how we failed to live up to our own earlier ambitions, still we all have to try to make some progress with our books about D. H. Lawrence."*[18] Dyer's conclusions are only a beginning. To follow an interest out of the darkness is a trick, a small Band-Aid for a larger problem. What happens, I wonder, when the study is complete, the book published? How do we remind ourselves to start again?

Norman Mailer wrote, *"The private terror of the liberal spirit is*

---

18. Geoff Dyer, *Out of Sheer Rage* (North Point Press, 1999), 231.

invariably suicide, not murder." Hans' letter was not a cry for help, it was an angry wail. In the final act he would force the world to see that he was right. He wasn't, but he couldn't help himself; he wanted others to believe. By September 28, 2006, Hans Reiser had given up. He was haunted and trapped. Then, for some reason, Hans decided to fight, to "not back down" as he told Nina in one of many threatening emails he sent her. In court, he frequently smiles as his enemies are exposed on the stand. He laughs at all of the prosecutor's jokes. He sees Paul Hora as a worthy adversary. The trial gives his life meaning; no matter what happens, the world will hear the wrongs perpetrated against him.

This book begins with a suicidal urge. If I was going to kill myself anyway, I could write whatever I wanted. And that's what I started to do. And then I met Sean and I became curious about things and my curiosity kept me going. But my curiosity about Sean Sturgeon and Hans Reiser will end. I've been playing emotional Russian roulette. Life requires more than a series of projects to keep us busy. I want to finish this story, which is structured around the depths of my own psychic pain. But I don't want to stick my head in the oven with no guarantees. Hans waits in his cell, thinking through his defense like a puzzle, which once solved will set him free. I'm thinking through my own.

Patty lives above Pacific Heights and from her bedroom you can barely see the lights on top of the Golden Gate Bridge. I haven't called her since her birthday four months ago. When we were dating she wouldn't let me wear clothes in her apartment or sit on the furniture, so when I arrive I take my clothes off in the entryway beneath the portrait of her deceased husband.

She used to buy me things, decorations for my bedroom, women's panties and a camisol she wanted me to wear when I slept with her. We would go to restaurants and she would order for me. I wouldn't even look at the menu. And if I wanted a beer, or something else, I would ask permission first.

Patty ties me to the bed facedown and stuffs her panties in my mouth. She beats me first with a thick paddle and then a cane. I try to clear my mind and let the pain wrap around me, separate the individual welts. I like this feeling, this helplessness. I like knowing there's nothing I can do.

There's still at least a month left in the trial. Hans has been raising his hand in court, interrupting the proceedings. The judge reprimanded him in front of the jury. I've been making extra money filing reports for *20/20*. I call several times a day to tell them who the witnesses are, if any new information is presented. A producer at *20/20* told me *48 Hours* might do a book about the trial and get Sean to sign an exclusive agreement. She was making it up, hoping I would sabotage the competition. It was all just ugly. The trial has gone three months already. How much is enough time to decide whether or not a person should spend the rest of their life in jail? During breaks I sit in the bathroom and crush a small amount of Adderall on top of the toilet-paper dispenser, snorting it quietly while the bailiffs and lawyers wash their hands.

"Do you remember when I told you never to write about me and you agreed?" Patty asks. I shake my head. I turn to look but she's moved behind me and I can't see her, just the edge of a yellow dresser and the curtain drawn across the window. I hear her rummaging through some drawers. I know she doesn't like being written about but I can't remember that specific conversation. Did I really say I would never write about her? I remember when we were first together and she cut me with a scalpel. It was the first time I had ever been cut by someone, three quick slices along my left rib whose scars I can still see clearly. I begged her to stop and later begged her to cut me again. Other times she stuck me full of needles, making heart patterns on my chest. I had no idea my capacity for pain before meeting her. Over time, when we were dating other people, we would occasionally sleep together. She would scratch messages in my side with her fingernails or with pins along my legs for the next woman to see. I remember Miranda running her fingertips over the dried blood at the top of my thighs, not commenting on the large red letters spelling out *MY DIRTY WHORE.*

Patty and I didn't use safe words. We didn't play "safe, sane, and consensually." She told me to call her "daddy," and threatened to shave my head. Sometimes she hit me when she was angry, when we were just walking down the street. Then she started taking pills for her anger and she became someone else.

"I don't know why I allow you to keep hurting me," Patty says, sitting next to me on the bed. I wait, moving just enough that my shoulder is against her leg. She gets up and hits me again, much harder, then again. I stretch my fingers forward as she lays into me. It doesn't feel good anymore. I'm thinking about Lissette and my father and someone who said that a writer will always sell you out. I'm saturated with self-loathing. Why is she doing this? I want her to stop but instead she goes back to the paddle, the thick wood landing heavily on my back. I don't scream or make any noise.

When Patty is done she unties me but I don't move. I lie like I'm dead, like a fish deposited on the sand. She lies on top of me. I feel like I am all out of tears, though I haven't cried at all. My insides are dry. She walks me to the door and I get dressed. She watches me with something like a concerned smile. It's well past midnight and I can hear rain pattering. I don't have anything to say. We hug and kiss. Her lips, thick and healthy, are the best thing about her.

"You're getting skinny. You need to eat." I don't respond. She presses a finger against my ribs. "Don't ever call me," she says, "or try to contact me again."

"What are your issues with women?"

I'm talking to an editor from a large publishing house. She's offering to buy this book but I don't think I can accept.

"I don't know," I say. "I'd like to be in a relationship."

"That's not the impression I get."

I know what she's saying. The only answer I can imagine is that my desires override each other. My desire for a stable, loving relationship is canceled out by the urge to be hurt and humiliated. But even without these desires I would have to develop the same skills everybody else does: to trust, to commit, to enrich someone else's life. I would have to become consistent.

The editor reminds me of a nurse who treated me the time I was found sleeping in a hallway with my wrist sliced open. "Why would you do that?" she asked. I didn't bother to reply. I was fourteen. She was blond and pretty, her hair cut in a practical bob. I stared at her jaw and watched her throat move as she talked and taped my wound shut. I wanted to ask if she would take me home, to point out her hypocrisy. But I didn't so I never knew whether she might have said yes. That was my first morning as a ward of the court.

My trials went for years as the state battled my father for custody. Family First was the official policy of the Department of Children and Family Services, and caseworkers would meet with me in small rooms asking if I wouldn't rather be with my dad. I was intransigent. Before the hearings my father whispered to me outside the courtroom, "You killed your mother," something he still says in the notes he sends me. He wanted to provoke an outburst so the judge, the social workers, would see me out of control. But that didn't happen. I usually turn my rage inward. He was fighting on principle; he didn't like anybody pushing him around. There was no chance of me going home with him, I would have gone back to the streets instead. And I don't think he wanted me home. He had never reported me missing. Eventually my father stopped showing up for the hearings but before that I asked him for his new address and he said I would find out where he lived in due time. And I did.

An older friend drove me from Chicago's South Side into Evanston. We went up and down the streets looking for my dad's Town Car. His other car was a 1971 sky blue Cougar convertible with a white leather interior, a 351 Quickstart engine, and the original hubcaps featuring a large cat curling around a red, white, and blue number one.

We found the Lincoln parked on a residential street in front of a three-story house with big windows blasting light onto a porch with a broad wood swing and a full green lawn. The house was gigantic. Somewhere inside was my older sister, my stepmother, my new sister only a year old. Later my father and I would make up and I would go in their kitchen and make sandwiches, even do my laundry, but I would never spend the night in that house.

I was fifteen years old. We were two blocks off the lake. If we listened we might have heard the surf bubbling onto the sand. The beaches were semi-private; residents were given tokens for admission, everybody else had to pay a fee. I sat with my friend for moments, or minutes, pretending it was no big deal that I had just found my father's house. Unsure of my own feelings, even to this day. Unsure if I had killed my mother. It seems impossible. I wasn't even there when she died. I didn't see her that morning, I just got up and went to school. And that day, summer just over, my father waited in the convertible with the top down, parked in front of the entrance in the early afternoon as we streamed from the building. The sky was as clear and blue as it's ever been. I climbed in the passenger seat without saying anything. He was crying for himself, hoping I might help him with his pain. But I was indifferent to it and didn't love him yet. I hadn't known my mother was dying. Nobody had said anything about that. Her death was simple; no arrests were made. She just didn't wake up. Her skin was bleached from years spent out of the sun, and the blood sifted through her and settled on her side in one large, colorful bruise. Or so I was told.

Eighteen months later and my father had a new wife, a new child, and a new house. The house was nicer, the wife was healthier, the neighborhood was better. Did I want to go inside? I remember it perfectly, the vibrancy of the memory the only testimony to the meaning of the discovery. I knew where my father lived again and I knew where I lived twenty miles away in a group home with eight other boys. That particular group home was a very hard place and I never wanted to go back there. It was spring. It was night. Our pockets were filled with coins from robbing parking meters. I stepped outside and ran a key along the back door of my father's dark blue car. Then we drove away.

You tell me, I think, still holding the phone with the editor from the large publishing house, feeling the pressure of the nurse's thumb on my palm as she pulls the tape and my skin comes together, making for a cleaner scar. What is my problem with women? Tell me and I'll believe you.

CHAPTER 9

*March/April; Nina's Last Day; The Part about Susan
Grabowski; Things that Can Be Known; Cateyes;
Hans Reiser Lies on the Stand; What's Missing on the
Missing Hard Drives: The Verdict; In the Woods with
the Children at Night*

On September 3, 2006, Anthony Zografos stopped by on his
way out of town. He was Nina's last boyfriend. They'd been together since she left Sean in 2005. He was going camping for the
night with his ex-wife and children in Big Basin near Santa Cruz.
Unlike Hans and Nina, Anthony and his ex were still cordial,
for the sake of the kids, but Anthony's wife wasn't very fond of
Nina. She had hopes she would get back together with Anthony
and was jealous of the depth of the affection he had for Nina but
had never had for her. He waited several minutes on the door-
step. It was unplanned, this last stop, just another opportunity
to see her face. Nina came straight from the shower, her black
hair shiny and wet.

An hour later she took the children to the Berkeley Bowl for
lunch and sent Anthony a text while they were eating: *I'm sorry I
missed your calls my love. It's great that you stopped to say goodbye.*

When the children finished eating Nina piloted the cart past
the bright tables stacked with colorful hills of fruit and vegetables, bulk bins chock-full of nuts and granola, piles of individually

wrapped cheeses. The Berkeley Bowl is teeming with locally grown produce and meats from nearby ranches. The store represents not just the wealth of the area but the wealth of the northern California countryside, and there must have been a time when Nina went through this store and thought, *There is nothing like this in Russia.*

She bought $150 worth of groceries, enough for a week. The groceries would sit in the back of her minivan and rot. The minivan would be discovered on a secluded street just off the highway. Inspectors would find her purse in the van, along with all of her possessions except her keys. Someone will have removed the battery from her phone. A security camera captured the children playing near the register while Nina first asked for a take-home container, then lifted Cori into the basket, Lila riding below the cart. In her parting shot Nina enters the frame wearing flip-flops and a purple sundress. We see the side of her, her naked arm pushing the handle, then she's gone.

It's six and a half miles, an eighteen-minute drive, from the Berkeley Bowl to Hans' mother's house, where he'd been living since the separation. It's a large house high up in the hills by an enormous regional park. There are steep cliffs and miles of woods, but you wouldn't want to leave the trails, the whole place is filled with poison oak.

At 2:04 PM Nina made her final phone call to tell Hans she'd be there soon. Actually, it was supposed to be her weekend with the kids but Hans insisted it was his. "What should I do?" she had asked Anthony. She didn't want to pay more lawyer fees. He told her to split the weekend and avoid the fight. When Hans said he would not back down he meant it. Anyway, it was Labor Day weekend, there was no school on Monday. Hans' mother would be in Nevada until Tuesday.

Sometime before 2:30 Nina arrived at the house. She was almost half an hour late. Hans made macaroni and cheese for Nina and Lila and spaghetti for Cori. Nina told him they'd just eaten but Hans insisted. Hans didn't want her to go. They ate, then Hans sent the children downstairs. There was or wasn't yelling. The children gave conflicting statements at different times to different people.

"I'm going to marry Anthony," Nina said. "And I think you should be looking for someone else as well."

Hans didn't want to talk about that. He wanted to talk about custody of the children and Nina's recent deposition taken by his new divorce lawyer, his sixth counting himself, in two years.

"You're not going to keep getting child support," Hans told her. "Because you did so poorly on your deposition. Actually, you should pay back some of the alimony I already gave you."

Nina listened patiently. She was used to Hans refusing responsibility, blaming his actions on the inconsiderateness of others. In his mind he never started it; he only responded. Hans tried to convince her to give up legal custody of the children, which she refused. He said Cori was bored at school and wanted to live with him. Nina said he was creating an unnecessary conflict for the child when he asked Cori to choose sides. Hans said he wanted Cori to see his dentist, which Nina said was fine. He thought if he kept talking he would wear her down. It always worked with his mother. If he just kept insisting his mother always gave up. But Nina didn't give up. She wouldn't let Hans have legal custody of the children. He warned her she would be convicted of embezzlement, of fraud. They were going to subpoena Sean's financial documents and the truth would come out that Nina and Sean were stealing from him. She nodded calmly, unconcerned.

Finally, after an hour, Nina said, "Hans, I have to go."

It was almost 4 PM. Nina called the children upstairs. Cori wrapped his arms around her waist, squeezing as hard as he could. He didn't kiss her because he had cavities and was afraid they might be contagious. Then Nina walked outside, or she didn't. The children watched her, or they went back downstairs. She walked up the stairs along the side of the house to the street, which was level with the top floor, the rest of the house built along a hill three stories below the road. Hans watched her walk away and felt a strange mix of desire and sadness. The sun on the back of Nina's legs, her ankles lifting from her sandals. He thought she looked magnificent. Hans thinks the only people who win in a divorce are the lawyers. He had wanted to tell her, when they were sitting on the couch, that they could wipe the slate clean. But she was so smug, so calm. Perhaps things would have been different if she had shown a little fear.

Here is where time fractures. Every unknown minute hanging like a string of question marks. Between 3:30 PM and 6:00 PM Nina said her last words, whatever they were. Maybe they weren't words at all, just a surprised gurgle and a look of terror. Maybe she made a threat, struggled, tried to bite. Perhaps she worked her fingers between someone's forearm and her neck, or wrapped her hands around someone's wrist, the blood vessels surrounding her eyes exploding like fireworks as she stared into the face of her killer. Perhaps the children were downstairs playing on the computers with the sound turned up when Nina was dragged back inside, the arm across her throat locking out the scream, her blood spraying against the beam in the center of the living room. Maybe she stepped into the van parked at the top of the driveway in front of Hans' mother's house, pushed her hair back, took the battery out of her phone, rested her purse on the floor in front of the passenger seat, slid the key into the ignition . . .

The day before Hans Reiser finally takes the stand to explain his side of the story, Susan Grabowski is found dead from a heroin overdose. We used to meet at the canal when I was a runaway, and later when I was in the homes. She was one of the only girls around. She was blond and pretty but with bad skin. She wore blue jeans and rock shirts, hooded sweaters beneath denim jackets. The same things we all wore. She lived on the western edge of the city and went to the technical high school but caught buses into Rogers Park. I'd seen her only a couple of times in recent years when she showed up at readings I did in Chicago. She was chubbier, and suffering from back problems, but otherwise seemed the same. The back problems came from an injury she'd suffered on the job. The heroin took away the pain and the settlement paid for the addiction.

My friends want to know if I'm coming for Susan's wake. After all, I was there for Mike's funeral. I weigh the pros and cons. There's a storm coming through the Midwest, and flights are delayed. It would have to be a quick trip, less than twenty-four hours, so as not to miss any of Hans' testimony. It would cost money, that's the thing. I'm putting a price tag on Susan's life. Is she worth more or less than $400 and six hours in a plane? I tell them I'm not coming. It's expensive to fly to Chicago, and Susan and I weren't close anymore.

I'm tired of my old friends dying. I don't know anyone in San Francisco who has lost four close childhood friends to drugs and suicide in the past six years. I keep wondering what it proves. It didn't seem consequential at the time. We were just getting high and keeping each other company before moving on to other things. I remember showing up for a fight at the grammar school and gazing across a sea of blue jackets and torn jeans. There must have been forty of us, not a single child with both parents living in the same home, and whoever we were supposed to fight got a glimpse of our numbers and turned away. It was an average, middle-class neighborhood. Why did we end up at the bottom of it? Why did we have to find each other? We were supposed to turn out OK and we didn't. There are no coincidences once you're dealing with percentages.

Hans' father hangs out in the vestibule the days before his son takes the stand. He was absent most of Hans' childhood, only coming back into Hans' life in the past ten years. He joined his son in Russia, where he says he was robbed by "a superbly conditioned crack addict." Called to testify by the defense, he says he warned his son in the weeks after Nina disappeared that the people following him were "KGB or S/M techno-geeks, probably the latter." During recess Hans' father does one-armed push-ups in the courtroom. He has an awkward, wanting smile. He might as well be saying, *I'm sorry but it's not my fault. Obviously, I'm paranoid and crazy. Don't blame me.*

If Hans Reiser, a strange kid with an absent father, had grown up in West Rogers Park, there is no doubt he would have been one of us. Now our numbers are thinning. We're marginalized. Until the last shot makes its final lap through our arteries, nobody knows for sure what's true. When we die our argument dies with us. The argument we never articulated well enough, that we were failed by our parents, and the schools, and the state. The cause of death is the missing safety net.

Nietzsche said there are no facts, only interpretations. Nina Reiser was five feet five inches tall and weighed 114 pounds. She was the mother of Cori and Lila. She met Hans through a bride service in St. Petersburg, Russia. These are facts. There are things that can be known.

I know I entered the mental hospital August 31, 1986, and was released three months later into the McCormick House, where I shared a room with Cateyes, a member of an all-black gang called the Vice Lords. These are facts. He tattooed a dagger on my left shoulder, which I later covered up with a larger, more colorful tattoo. He called himself Cateyes because of his large green eyes that pinched slightly at the corners toward his ears. But he wore thick glasses and his eyesight was getting worse. No one paid attention or cared enough to try and figure out why his sight was deteriorating. He wasn't in touch with any family except his brother, also a gang member, also living in a state-run home.

Cateyes slept with the radio playing beneath his pillow. "I dare you to turn it off," he said. It didn't matter; I was too afraid to sleep. Sometimes I slept in the bathroom with the door locked.

I shook when Cateyes made a fist and jerked his shoulders sharply. "It's OK," Big John told me. "There's nothing wrong with being scared." But there was everything wrong with being scared. I lost coordination in my arms and legs. I couldn't defend myself. I was food waiting to be eaten.

Cateyes was four years older than I was and the worst kind of inconsistent friend. Sometimes I sat with him in the homework room tutoring him in math or history as he studied for his GED. They called me Einstein in that home because I would figure out how much Night Train or Mad Dog it would take to equal a pint of vodka or a six-pack of beer. Away from the home, if there was trouble, Cateyes would protect me. Hours later, back at McCormick House, he would stand over me as I sat paralyzed on the edge of the mattress while he smacked his palm, showing off his power over me, and called out to one of the other kids, "Hey, Jerry. Come here. Check this out."

It was the time of Harold Washington, Chicago's first black mayor, and there was construction all over the South Side where we lived. There were bunting ribbons in front of buildings and blue and white signs with the mayor's name. Washington actually lived in the same neighborhood, just closer to the lake. Farrakhan's mosque was also nearby. So was Jesse Jackson and the Rainbow Coalition. Jackson hosted cultural conversations at Operation PUSH headquarters. Farrakhan's house was on Woodlawn and quiet men, wearing mirrored sunglasses and suits with bow ties, stood watch in front on the grass. But we didn't pay attention to any of that. Every week in McCormick House we piled into the van and the staff took us to the bowling alley at the Circle Campus. We would bowl, or they would give us $2 to play quarter video games. Coming home we would stop for Polish sausages and strawberry sodas at Maxwell and Halsted. House music was rising from the ground in 1986. It was a new kind of music with pounding bass, drum machines, samples, and repetitive phrases. It was music stolen from other music and changed, like a hot-wired car on blocks at the chop shop getting new rims and a paint job. The sound was raw and melodic and could keep you dancing for hours. It was a movement flowering in the Chicago ghetto, championed by Frankie Knuckles and Trax Records. We didn't know we were at the center of a national storm, that our music was spreading like an oil spill toward Detroit. We listened to the beats as we drove to and from Circle Campus. One day the van began to drive away and Cateyes wasn't inside. We were dancing to the new tunes, everybody pounding on the seats. Our favorite staff member, Kev, a former gang member himself, was driving and saying, "Do it now. Do it." And there was Cateyes running to catch up. He was so fast, running down the middle of the street, cutting between cars. Kev kept driving. "Look at him run."

"C'mon Cateyes!"

Cateyes jumped into the van, sweating, smiling, everybody patting him on the back and he's singing along. He knew the music better than anybody.

I remember the crowd near Cateyes' dresser at the end of spring as he pulled off his shirt, his skin an even brown like toffee, a few tightly curled black hairs on his chest. His body was muscular, sensual, his wide back tapering neatly to his waist. He took off his thick glasses, sat them on top of the dresser, grabbed the tip of his nose with two fingers, shook his head in disbelief. He had been caught stealing by Michael, the other white kid in the home. Michael had been through Cateyes' things. Now we waited. Cateyes swung his fist into Michael's mouth and the group expanded to accommodate the violence as it spilled into the hallway. I don't remember how long the fight lasted or what happened next. I remember the punch was perfect.

Here's a fact: Cateyes went blind. When he was too old to live in McCormick he moved into the YMCA, tapping a path around the Near West Side just past the Greyhound Station. He was given a six-month independent living allowance. Then he was homeless. Then he died. It was cancer behind his eyes. The cancer was making him blind. Already, when we were roommates, his lenses thick as Coke bottles while the cancer did its work. But nobody bothered to check. He was twenty-three.

Hans Reiser created a file system to reorganize information. There are facts, but we can present them in any order we want. Here is a fact: against his attorney's advice Hans Reiser takes the stand. Here is another fact: Hans Reiser was the last known person to see Nina alive.

The first thing Hans did when told his estranged wife was missing was spend half an hour hosing down his driveway. The cherry blossoms and leaves covered the pavement and he stood in one place, the hose hanging limply in his hand, spraying a small circle of pavement. The next morning he went to see his lawyer. His lawyer said he needed a criminal attorney and referred him to Bill Du Bois. On September 7, forty-eight hours after Nina was reported missing, Hans met Du Bois for the first time and gave him a $5,000 retainer. The police were calling but he never answered the phone. He never returned Nina's mother's calls. He never called Nina to see if she'd been found. He never got the chance to say, "I'm glad you're OK. You almost cost me $5,000."

Hans' testimony begins March 5, 2008, and lasts eleven days, spread over a month to allow a vacation for the judge and jury. Unlike the phone call he made to his mother during which he spoke of Nina in the past tense, on the stand he speaks of Nina in the present tense. He says, "Nina has the most beautiful voice of any woman I've ever met. She's very perceptive, that's one of her gifts. I remember thinking women like her aren't interested in me and now I wonder if maybe I should have understood that. She said she loved me but when you look at it objectively it's hard to come to that conclusion."

He talks about meeting Nina. It was a time when it looked like Russia was going democratic, before they tried to return the statue of Felix Dzerzhinsky to Moscow Square. He liked living with her then but she didn't like living with him. Du Bois asks why that was and Hans says, "She wouldn't go to bed until everything was put away. I would just sort of leave things."

"In 2000," Hans says, "Nina was having depression issues. There was this artist in Moscow who draws pictures of people on T-shirts. This is a real artist I'm talking about and the picture he drew of Nina was really a shock. It was an extremely neurotic, unhappy Nina that he drew."

Hans catalogs all the things he dislikes about Nina. His anger shines through as if she left him yesterday. Nothing galls him more than how much other people liked her. "She works people," he says. "She complimented the teachers. She even stroked their hands." He remembers her rubbing a fat man's stomach and saying, "There's nothing but muscle here."

The picture he paints is of a patient, considerate woman who enjoys making other people smile. But that's not what Hans sees. He has no idea how he's being perceived. He has no idea what the artist saw in Nina on the street in Moscow in 2000.

In a letter to Alameda County Supervisor Gail Steele written in June 2006, Hans recommended sweeping changes to child protective services and the court's supervisory function in custody disputes. The court had sided consistently with Nina, awarding her full legal custody of the children. The only chance Hans had left was to rearrange the system in his favor, which was no chance at all. He wrote, *"This could end up being more important than my two decades of work in computer science, if you decide to back it."* The letter is many pages long, paranoid, narcissistic. He felt unjustly punished by the state and asked rhetorically, *"Does inaccurate punishment damage the psychology of those punished, and increase the likelihood of later real domestic violence?"*

Under cross-exam Hans is unable to account for any of his actions following Nina's disappearance. He either doesn't answer or he lies. When his mother returned from Burning Man, Hans had cleaned the house, something he had never done before. He had also never cleaned the car, but this time he did. He says he cleaned the car to please his mother but then he hid the car from her and wouldn't give it back. Then he changes his testimony to say that he cleaned the car because it smelled of spilled milk. He cleaned the car by filling it with an inch of water. He says he thought there was a drainage hole, but there wasn't. He says there was a drainage hole in the floor of his previous car, but that turns out not to be true.

Before he was told Nina was missing, Hans showed up at his kids' school saying he wanted to put his mother's name on the pickup list, but she was already on the pickup list. He left the school his phone number, in case of emergency, but the number he left was wrong. On Friday, September 8, for the first time, Hans engaged in countersurveillance. He drove onto the highway, got off, got back on going the other way, slowed down, sped up, parked by the side of the road, then pulled out again. He wanted to know if he was being followed, and he was. He says he was feeling paranoid because the day before a man had approached him at the school and offered to watch his children.

On the stand he recites the license plate number of the officer who followed him five days after the murder, but can't remember other, more basic things. He can't remember where he was when he removed the passenger seat from the car and he can't remember where he threw it away. He says he threw it away instead of storing it at his mother's house because his mother was trying to get custody of Cori and Lila and he wasn't allowed to be there. But he went there almost every day, and slept at her house at least three times that week. He also removed the rear assembly from the car and threw that away. He says he was going to fill it in with futon foam and bring his mother her new, fixed-up car, a bed on four wheels.

None of his testimony adds up. He says he didn't call Nina to find out why she didn't pick up the children because he wasn't supposed to call her. But he had called her twenty-six times the month before. Once he called her three times in ten minutes. He says he withdrew $10,000 from banks and ATMs because of a new policy his credit union had instituted, charging a fee for cash advances on credit cards. But the new policy had actually gone into effect more than a year earlier. He says he was not in the habit of removing the battery from his phone, then admits that was a lie.

"You willfully concealed the fact that you had removed the battery from your phone?" Hora asks.

"Yes," Hans replies. "And I feel badly about that."

He drove almost two hours outside of Oakland to examine storage lockers big enough to hide the car and priced out a one-way U-Haul back to the city. He says he wanted to live in the storage locker, seventy-five miles away from his children and his business. He stayed in campgrounds two hours from his home and denies knowing there was a campground just a mile away from the house he lived in for thirty years. He says he was sleeping in his car and went to the campgrounds to shower. But he had a membership at 24 Hour Fitness.

He tells the jury it's important to understand that since the divorce, Nina liked Lila more than Cori. This is the most important thing. If they understand this, they'll understand everything. His testimony is bizarre, rambling. He objects. He answers questions he isn't asked. He answers questions with questions, just as Sean had with me. He says, "All my life people have been doing things. Like in grade school kids would pick on me. They would chase me. I've been losing social interactions all my life . . . I can't communicate effectively because that's not how scientists talk. I have a habit; I have a compulsive tendency to say things that I know are true, that people do not want to be true. If you tell people things they don't want to hear, they don't like you for it. If you prove it, they hate you even more. I realize now all my problems were caused by not looking people in the eye. A third of the population can be vicious to me. It had been building and building. I'd been losing all these social battles. And then they took away [my children] the only important thing to me. And the facts didn't matter. They just didn't matter."

"Why did you remove the hard drives from your computer?" Paul Hora asks.

"I didn't want the police to take them. I was the subject of a murder investigation."

"You said you removed the hard drives on the seventh. Why did you think she was murdered on September 7? She was missing. You just heard she was missing on the night of September 5. Didn't you think she might have had an accident, that she could be in the hospital? Why would you think it was murder?"

"You've convinced me," Hans replies. "It must have been the eighth."

During closing arguments Hora walks the jury through the crime. He places a puzzle on an easel next to a picture of Nina. Every piece contains a clue: the missing hard drive, Nina's last location, Hans' active cover-up. Hora presents a clear narrative for the jury, from the importance of Nina leaving her children, to Hans' motives, to

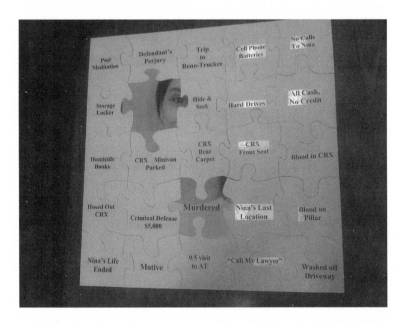

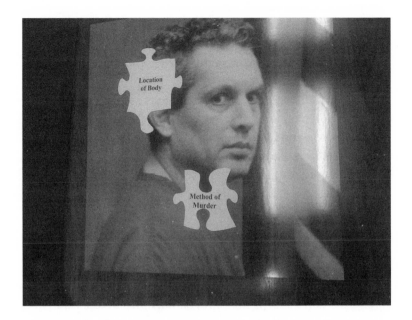

his lies on the stand. Each time Hora removes a piece of the puzzle he places it over Nina, revealing Hans, until the only pieces
left are the location of the body and the method of murder.

Hora asks the jury, "If you were innocent, why wouldn't you
offer to help? Why would you refuse to talk to the police when
your wife is missing, and immediately contact your lawyer?"
Pointing at Hans, Hora continues, "He says he spilled milk in the
car before his mother went to Burning Man. If you spill milk in
the car you don't throw away sections of the car. You don't throw
large portions of your car away when your wife is missing and you
think you're being investigated for a homicide. Then he [Hans]
took it a step further, says 'I've always wanted to build a futon in
the back of the car.' Why wait until your wife's missing to build
a futon in the back of your mom's car?" Paul talks about the cell
phones, how when Nina's phone was recovered the battery was
missing, just as Hans' battery was missing from his phone when
he was arrested.

"Two hundred seventy thousand people drive across the Oakland Bay Bridge every day," Hora says, displaying an image of the bridge on the screen. "If you stopped every single one of them, how long do you think you would have to wait to find one of them with the battery intentionally taken out of his phone? How many years would you have to wait to find one with the battery out of his phone and the front seat removed from his car?"

Du Bois follows Hora. "This has been a tough case for me," he says. "Because my client is a difficult person to communicate with, to relate to, to present as a witness. Nina is easy to like and likeable, a pleasure to look at, a pleasure to be around." He talks about the evidence in the order it was presented, trying to punch tiny holes in each of the sixty witnesses' testimonies. "Do you really think Officer Denson, a trained police officer with twenty-seven years' experience, would tell Nina to buy a gun?" He doesn't link the evidence into a story and perhaps that's intentional. He wants to remove the file system, to make it impossible to structure the information. He talks a lot about the things that are unknown. What evidence was Hans hiding when he hosed down the driveway? What evidence was supposedly on the car seat Hans threw away? And why didn't the prosecution call Sean Sturgeon? He projects a platypus onto the evidence screen. "The platypus is odd. Hans is odd. Odd in the way he speaks. Odd in the way he carries himself. Hans Reiser is the duck-billed platypus amongst normal people and gets the same consideration, under the law, as you and I."

"If the platypus doesn't fit, you must acquit," I whisper to the producer seated next to me.

"You should use that in your book," she says.

In the morning I take ten milligrams of Adderall and then ten more of the extended release. I sit down in the coffee shop then go into the bathroom and snort a few more lines. I thought I had stopped snorting Adderall, but I keep coming back to it. In the 1950s when Dexadrine and Dexamyl and other amphetamine combinations were being mass consumed as diet pills, research started coming out about tolerance and the return of lost weight. When the National Academy of Sciences advised the FDA that amphetamine weight loss products were not very effective, the pharmaceutical companies suppressed the information for years.[19] Now Lindsay Lohan and Nicole Ritchie are taking Adderall for weight loss like the fifties housewives, because it's the same thing. The amphetamine hasn't changed. Benzedrine, Dexedrine, methamphetamine. They're all forms of beta-phenyl-isopropylamine: synthetic adrenaline.

The closing arguments are over and I bicycle through the city. All the pot clubs are open at night, their unlocked doors throwing green light onto the streets. I pass the line of bike messengers waiting to get into the Zeitgeist for a cold beer. I bike Valencia, Guererro, Dolores. These streets are noisy, crowded. This is where I live, in the city that I arrived at accidentally. It's good to have a home, to know I'm going to be here for a while. That I'll stay where I am, sharing a one-bedroom apartment close to the park and the coffee shop I like, in the middle of everything, with my young roommate, for as long as I can.

"Little kids need their mother," Paul Hora said in his summation. "Little kids miss their mother. He [Hans] hid her body. Hiding the body is so much worse. The pain and suffering you cause those kids for life. They never get to have a funeral or visit a headstone."

Du Bois countered by saying the prosecution had not proven its case. He said the burden of evidence against the accused has

---

19. Nicolas Rasmussen, *On Speed: The Many Lives of Amphetamine* (New York: New York University, 2008), 166.

been getting lighter in recent years. He talked about prisoners freed after serving decades for crimes they didn't commit. He talked about George W. Bush and his case for war, Colin Powell going to the United Nations with stories of weapons of mass destruction. It was the most, perhaps only, compelling part of Du Bois' case. But it wasn't enough for me. I believed the father was guilty. I agreed with Hora, little kids need their mother.

For the last two months I've been dating three women. They all have different partners and know about each other. I met them all at almost the same time and see each a couple times a week. There's Caterina who lives with her boyfriend and works in Oakland. She has spikey blond hair, a mousy nose, and dresses like a boy. We grab lunch together and occasionally in the evening she comes over with her boyfriend and the three of us have dinner. Her boyfriend brings me flowers. Caterina and I don't have sex or do S/M, we just kiss and talk. We sit near the fountain in downtown Oakland by the bubble tea stand, my legs over her legs, her hand on the back of my neck.

And there's Mary, who is young and soft with smooth, comforting curves. She works at the bakery on the corner and sleeps over when she has to be at work early. She likes it when I wear the camisole and panties Patty bought me and I sleep in front of her on the inside of the spoon.

There's also Raina, a nurse's aide who does fetish modeling and porn films. Raina has lots of partners, dominant and submissive. She's what people in the S/M community refer to as "lifestyle" and what that really means is that sadomasochism is at the center of her world. In her teens she was homeless and by her early twenties she was addicted to heroin. Now, in her late twenties, she's mostly got herself together. She's self-educated and reads a book every day. She's a heavy player, like Sean used to be, and her legs are often covered in large bruises. I'm not a heavy player. I usually can't take that much pain. But I like being marked and

I'm emotional and very submissive around the right person. I get shy and I think about the worst things I've experienced and I let the chains and the belts lift those things off of me, at least for a little while. All my fears and failures dissipate. Like the fear of my father when he dragged me home one night in the winter of 1985. His large, dark car slid toward the curb and came to a halt. "Get in," he said. We drove home in silence and walked into the house and his face tensed up and he smacked me so hard I fell against the wall. I had just turned fourteen and my father was big and muscular. But that's not what matters. He wasn't really that much bigger than me, he just seemed that way because he had been screaming at me all my life. What matters, the only thing that matters at all, is that I didn't fight back. I froze, the way my father froze that day in 1970 when the man ran up to him in the park and said, "Did you hit my kid?" That kid he was referring to was my age, but my father couldn't protect me from the man hitting me. My father *was* that man and I was my father's son and he handed his fear down to me. He gave me an opportunity to correct his failure and I passed on it. None of it would have mattered if I fought back, but I didn't. If I had, both of our lives would have been different.

When I'm tied up, it's the woman's responsibility to protect me. She becomes my mother and my father. She gets angry for reasons I can't understand, but she doesn't leave. I absorb her anger, which becomes forgiveness. She stands behind my bed, then leans over me, her belly pressing against my face. I'm inhaling her stomach while she digs her nails into my skin. We're standing at the intersection of our desires. What she wants is to be needed and to take control and what I want is to need and give up control. She hogties me on my bedroom floor, lining clothespins along my chest and thighs. She turns me over and lies on top of me. There are times when the pain is so great and I close my eyes and see my father grimacing behind a curtain of snow and because I can't fail, because now I am thirty-six years old and there is nothing I can do, the tears pour from my face. She is Lissette, she is Raina, she is Patty, she is so many others. She is my savior and addiction and she says, "I think you're wonderful." She says, "I think you're amazing." She takes in my failures and my shortcomings, and she loves me the way only a mother can love a child. The pain takes away everything else. It's as if she's dug a finger through my ribs and is scratching at my heart. The euphoria spreads into a smile so large that I am almost laughing too. And I say, "I love you." I tell my mother I love her as she wraps her hand around my penis and shushes me and says all these things that my body is telling me, they're all OK. They're part of my beauty, part of who I am, even the fear. She says, "To me you are perfect. I wouldn't want you any other way."

"You don't have to be embarrassed around me," Raina says. I'm lying with my head in her lap, my legs wrapped around her waist, naked as a baby. She's stroking my hair. "I've seen everything. There's nothing you could do that would freak me out. I already understand how fucked up you are."

Mary, Caterina, and Raina have all met each other. They come to readings I have in the city and send each other their regards. It sounds ridiculous and complex, and it probably is. But actually, I'm as relaxed and happy as I've been in a while. Summer is coming and the sky is blue almost every day. The jury will reach its verdict. The park near my house fills with people and I don't feel lonely. Caterina tells me to try and enjoy it.

"You're surrounded by people who like you," she says. But she lives with her boyfriend. They've been together six years. And before that she was married.

"Right," I say. "But I'd like some guarantees."

And even in the best of times I don't always keep it together. Raina is in my bedroom. I'm blindfolded and dressed like a girl and bleeding a little from some of the things she's been doing.

"I'm going to wash my hands," she says.

"Don't go," I almost scream, wrapping my arms around her leg. The panic shoots through me, turning to a cold, familiar fear. *I'll never see her again.* "I'm sorry," I say. I say it over and over and over. "I'm sorry. I'm sorry. I'm sorry."

"I'm not going anywhere," Raina says, almost singing. "I'm staying right here."

The jury goes into deliberations and we're all sent home to wait for the call. I collect $5 from six journalists and start a pool to guess when the verdict will arrive. One day stretches into two, and then a long weekend. The jury asks for several pieces of evidence, but the court won't relay their requests to the media. On Monday I go for a ride along the bay, bicycling slowly past the docks and under the bridge and the old boats out near Hunters Point that seem never to have moved in the ten years I've lived here. There are people living in this area and they're angry because the city ignores them, the streets aren't maintained, there's too much crime. On the upcoming ballot there's an initiative that will transform the entire neighborhood with luxury condos and wide streets and green parks, and all the angry residents that don't already own property will have to go somewhere else.

I've been contracting with *20/20* for almost six months. Part of the deal is that I'm supposed to do an on-camera interview when the trial is over. I thought they wanted to talk to me about Hans but what they're really interested in is Sean. They want me to talk about sadomasochism while they cut away to fuzzy images of women wearing leather, handcuffs on bedsheets, whips. They want to make a link between sadomasochism and death. But if anything became clear in this trial it's that kinky sex had nothing to do with it.

The *20/20* producers called me as a group and put me on speaker phone. They told me the questions they were going to ask about Sean. They wanted me to explain the difference between a bottom, a top, and a switch. They wanted me to talk about Sean as a "heavy player" and the kind of things Sean might like. The facts are correct but the questions are wrong, too sensational and out of context. I'm writing about the same things in my own book but I don't trust these people.

"Why not just ask me about the trial?" I said. "I've been in court every day. I know this case better than anyone."

"Oh please," the senior producer said. "You can't really pretend you didn't know we would ask you about this."

"I need to think about it," I said.

"Oh, Stephen," she replied. "I'm so disappointed in you."

I turn off the Bay, along Sixteenth Street, toward the base of Portero Hill. *We have an agreement. I'm so disappointed in you.* They don't even try to mask their manipulation. Then they call back. The jury has reached a verdict.

"You're too late," a woman tells me on the first floor of the courthouse. It's one of the producers from *20/20*. She's pregnant with twins and she's waiting near the information desk, hoping to catch some jurors on their way out.

I bolt up the stairs and emerge from the fifth-floor stairwell into a scrim of boom mikes and tripods. The vestibule is packed to the walls with local and national media outlets. In the short hallway to the restroom the video techs are replaying the verdict on the double monitor. The on-air talent are already relaying their stories back to the viewing audience, the cameramen wrangling long coils of electrical cord. I crouch beneath the water fountains, near the machine where the professionals re-dub beta tapes. There are agreements already in place between broadcasting companies for pool cameras. The producers are whispering, trying to keep secrets from each other. The union crews hustle to stay busy and earn a spot on the next job. I'm thankful for their monitors, two small screens sitting on top of the series of beams with wheels full of media decks, cassettes popping out like toaster waffles.

It's the first time Goodman has allowed cameras in his courtroom, one in the front row of the gallery, another from the witness stand, staring at all the participants. I ignore what's going on around me and focus instead on the screen: inside Courtroom Nine every seat is taken and a large crowd stands back near the doors. The bailiffs make no move to clear people who were unable to find seats. Hans, Du Bois, and Hora sit at the long table in the center. Du Bois is sad, his cheeks seeming to slide from his jaw, eyes drawn and bewildered. He knows the jury is coming back too soon. Hans looks like he was yanked out of bed, the top button undone on his shirt, his thick red tie hanging loosely from his collar, begging to be tightened. He leans toward Du Bois, whispering in his ear as the jury files behind them, settling into two rows of seats out of view of the cameras facing the accused.

Juror Number One is chosen as the foreman. I remember him listening closely during Cori's testimony, nodding and encouraging the boy, smiling thoughtfully as the child squirmed uncomfortably on the stand. He gives the bailiff a note, which the bailiff then walks over to Judge Goodman. The judge opens the envelope, reads it, hands it back to the bailiff. The bailiff returns the note to the foreman.

"Does that represent your true and final verdict?" Goodman asks. Each juror says yes in their turn. Murder in the first degree, pre-meditated, with malice.

"Bailiff, remove Mr. Reiser from the courtroom." I shift from one leg to another while watching. There's commotion behind me, heels clicking rapidly against the linoleum, but on the screen the court is stunned silent.

"I've been the best father that I know how," Hans says. He has more to say but he doesn't get the chance. The bailiff taps him on the shoulder, grips his arm at the elbow and wrist, pulls him from the room. He will no longer be granted the courtesy of the accused.

The holding cell door closes in front of Hans, his mouth still open. The judge thanks the jury for their service. The camera focuses on Paul Hora leaning back at the table, folding his hands together. Du Bois shuffles a folder into a briefcase.

I watch the verdict again, but now from another angle, the view from the witness stand. Each juror answers affirmatively. This case has aged Du Bois. He's a highly regarded defense attorney and I've come to like him immensely, even if I never believe a word he says. The camera drops to an empty trash bin beneath the table, a bag folded loosely around its rim, then rises again to his face. Then Hans. Hans looks stunned as the clerk reads, "We the jury find the defendant guilty of murder. On or about September 3, 2006, in the county of Alameda, Hans Reiser did and with malice murder Nina Reiser."

"I've been the best father that I know how." The bailiff stands ready behind Hans, taps him on the shoulder, leads him forcefully from the room.

"Can you rewind?" I say. "Play it again?"

There are press conferences. Du Bois promises appeals; Hora says justice has been served. The jurors slip out a side door. Late in the afternoon the building is mostly empty. I look in on Courtroom Nine. Boxes of tapes, documents, and displays sit at the front of the room. The jury hardly requested any of it. Now it will have to be stored somewhere, the transcripts of phone calls Hans made to his mother and pleading voice mails left for Nina; the photographs of Nina and the children and her blood sprayed across the beam; swabs, DNA lab results; recordings, videos; maps charting Hans' routes through the East Bay as he tried to evade the police; receipts for a water pump, for books about murder; testimony from social workers, doctors; financial records; everything that went into the story Paul Hora wrote for the jury having served its purpose.

I meet a friend near the courthouse. She's a professor of political science at Berkeley. We drive south and find a restaurant in a residential district nestled between the hills and the freeway leading onto the bridge. I have a beer, then another. I tell her what Hans said, his last words before he was led away, "He said, 'I've been the best father that I know how.'"

"By killing their mother?" she asks.

"It was as if he was talking to me," I say.

"Does he know you're writing a book?"

"I doubt it."

Hillary Clinton is on the television above the bar. A scroll runs below her chin, repeating an earlier statement about what would happen to Iran if Israel were attacked. She says, "Iran would be obliterated." It's nearing the end of the Democratic primaries and it occurs to me that for the last five and a half months I've hardly thought about anything except Hans Reiser. I haven't been following the news or playing cards. For more than two years I went to my friends' house every Sunday night to watch television. But during the trial my friends had a baby and we stopped doing that. I saw the baby once and I held her awkwardly, terrified I'd drop her as she made circles with her tiny mouth. She was a colicky baby but recently she's stopped crying. The trial is over.

"You seem excited," my friend says. We're outside on the sidewalk near an ice-cream shop and a closed-down bookstore. There are lots of lights and teenagers everywhere.

In the morning I'm back in court, mildly hungover. Hans is there but doesn't get to say anything. The judge schedules the sentencing. Murder one is a mandatory twenty-five years to life.

Du Bois asks for some words with his client. The two men lean toward each other, like lovers. They pat each other's arms, whispering. Hans spreads his fingers over Du Bois' shoulder, reassuring him, until Hans is taken from the room and returned to his cell.

"What now?" I say to one of the reporters.

"I'm so glad to be done with this bullshit," he replies.

When Hans said, "I've been the best father I know how," he meant that he did it for his children, more specifically his son. I remember his testimony, the thing the jury absolutely had to know, was that Nina didn't love Cori after the divorce. He interrupted his own lawyer to say that when Nina informed him she was leaving, she also switched her affection from Cori to Lila. Hans said it was important to understand that Nina changed this way, otherwise it would seem like he was contradicting himself and nothing would add up. None of us knew what he was talking about. I shook my head and whispered to one of the journalists, "What is he referring to?"

"He's gone off the rails," he whispered back. But we were wrong. We were ignoring something consequential: the lattice of justifications a murderer assembles as he builds toward the crime.

In one of the key pieces of evidence, the wiretapped phone call to his mother three weeks after Nina was murdered, Hans said, *"She came up with these illnesses for Cori because she hated me . . . Cori understands his mother wants him to be sick and doesn't really like him on some deep, conflicted level."* Hans sounded tired in that call, depressed, explaining to his mother that Nina was killing his son.

On Friday, September 1, the last weekday before he killed Nina, Hans called District Supervisor Gail Steele. He wanted to know what she thought of his proposal to overhaul the child welfare system. Hans was certain the supervisor would take his proposal seriously. He had donated $2,000 to her campaign. But after calling six times that week, four times that day, he never called her again. The bureaucracy would not bend to his will so he took care of the problem himself.

He did it to save his son.

Except he didn't. Nina had been with Hans for five years. She knew Hans better than anybody and she left him for his only friend. This is the moment, Hans told the jury, when she ceased loving their son. In fact, it's the moment when Hans realizes Nina didn't love him, and that maybe she never did. His mind went searching for a reason. Surely she understood he was a famous computer programmer? Her rejection wasn't consistent with the

identity he had built for himself. He had to reorganize the data; it was too much to take and he gave it to his son to carry. When Hans said, "I've been the best father that I know how," he meant, "I killed the mother to save the boy."

When I asked my father why he moved while I was sleeping on the streets, he said I was a drug addict so he abandoned me for the good of the family. That was the story he put together. The opposite of the story I had put together about being an abused child. But some large part of me hadn't wanted things to work out with my father, even then. I despised him for screaming. I disapproved of the way he led his life. He never hit me until after I left home and brought shame on him. I rejected my father. There was only my father and my sister, and my sister would be in college soon. My grandparents were dead. My mother's family was in England. And my father moved and wouldn't tell me where he

went. The family my father left me for didn't exist. He was referring to the family he didn't yet have, the family coming soon, the
family hoped-for. Or not. He was referring to himself.

All systems of domination create stories of their own benevo-
lence. The imperialists arrive to tame the savages. We tie the
noose around Saddam Hussein's neck, place a bag over his head,
the floor swings open beneath his feet, and his dead body hangs
in the gallows. I was traveling with President Bush in 2004, three
days after the pictures were published of Abu Ghraib. He stood
near third base in a little league stadium and gave the same
speech he gave in every city. Except right in the middle of his
speech he slid in one extra sentence. He said, "Thanks to our actions, Saddam's torture chambers have been closed."

"Did he just say what I think he said?" I asked the local reporter next to me. The crowd cheered. They had no idea he was
saying this for the first time. They thought it was part of the
speech. But it wasn't. It was the official response to evidence to
the contrary.

Hans Reiser killed Nina because she rejected him, but he will
never know that. Something so selfish is beyond knowing. My father abandoned me to the streets because I had no forgiveness
in me. I was eleven, twelve, thirteen, fourteen, and I sat in judg-
ment of my father so he left me sleeping in some hallway and got
a new house. Those people in that stadium weren't concerned
with the picture of a soldier giving the thumbs-up next to the
body of a man packed in ice beaten to death by American soldiers. We were taking our revenge. Revenge for what? They rejected us, that's what. We respond with the violent indignation of
colonizers. We understand the world by how we retrieve memories, re-order information into stories to justify how we feel.

"Thanks to our actions Saddam's torture chambers are now
closed."

"I did it for the good of the family."

"I've been the best father that I know how."

On the night of September 4, one day after Nina was killed, Hans visited the Redwood Recreation Area with his two children. He testified he wanted to teach them not to be afraid of the dark.

Redwood, a giant park thick with trees and gullies and steep drops, stretches for miles, large enough to hike for days. The children were four and six and they didn't know that they would never see their mother again. He said he gave the children flashlights and told them to look for deer. They walked the fire road into the park, failing to notice the broken lock hanging from the gate. It must have been quiet except for the pebbles and twigs crunching beneath them and whatever wind was forcing its way through the hills. They didn't see any deer. An owl stared from its branch, unmoving, the beam crossing its feathers. On the stand Hans mentioned the owl three times.

Two hundred meters in Cori and Lila stopped. They were at the limits of their fear. There were trees on either side of them. The only light came from the flashlights held in their small hands. What if one of them dropped a flashlight, or one of the bulbs burned out? What if there are good reasons children are afraid of the dark? Why were they in the woods, pinned beneath a three-quarter moon? Years from now will the path open or will they remember the branches closing in on them? Hans Reiser marched through the woods with his children at night, the beams of light skittering across the branches, the owl and its disapproving beak watching, motionless. Most likely Hans was looking to see if Nina's grave was visible, or he was trying to clear his head. But the owl wasn't having it, and the children were afraid.

CHAPTER 10

May/June/July/August; The Attraction of Controlled Violence; Hans Changes His Story; Boxing Miranda; Sean Sturgeon's Confession; Threats in the Diner; False Prophets and Fierce Attachments; Father and Son

At a boxing match in the Tenderloin the fighters circle each other wearing thick gloves, large padded headgear, crotch protectors resembling rubber diapers on the outside of their shorts. It's an amateur bout, each fight lasts three two-minute rounds. Outside, a line of pedestrians forms on the street, staring through the bay windows.

I see Miranda near the entrance. Her earrings are gone, her clothes are less revealing, there are no gold streaks in her black curls. I almost hug her but as I approach she leans away as if she were afraid of getting sick. I ask how she's doing and she says fine. We talk for a moment about the upcoming state ballot. Large landlords are trying to end tenant protections, hiding their agenda under the guise of eminent domain reform. I've been getting political again, organizing events, printing flyers, and making T-shirts that say SAVE RENT CONTROL. Miranda says she's already involved with a group working on the same issue. Then she says something about getting a bottle of water and walks off.

I go back to my friends. People are screaming. There are an unusual number of beautiful women in the gym, unabashedly sexy, wearing tight shirts and pants, revealing as much skin as they can. They're fighters or girlfriends of the fighters, drawn to the pursuit of controlled violence. I see Miranda on the other side of the room, looking away. For ten months I've been sending her notes, calling her, but she never responds. I walk over to her again.

"What happened?" I ask. "I never heard from you after the Fourth of July."

"I didn't want to talk to you then, or now, or ever," she says.

"But why?"

I've said exactly the wrong thing. She stares through me with pure hatred. Or maybe I'm giving myself too much credit. Miranda pushes past me through the crowd toward the exit. I go back to the post in the middle of the gym and lean against it as the fighters beat each other with their large gloves and padded heads. At the end the fighters are drenched in sweat, barely moving. When asked why he liked using fighters as actors, David Mamet responded, *"Because fighters are sad."*[20]

---

20. *New York Times*, April 27, 2008.

I met Miranda at a literary festival where I read a story about a young adult stalking the man who molested him. At the end of the story the molester reminds the young man that he had also kept him safe. Nobody else had hurt him when he was around. He places his hand over the younger man's face and says, "I would do it again."

Wearing cheap black boots and a schoolgirl skirt that didn't cover her knees, she was standing in front of me when I came down from the stage. She had a tiny ring through her lower lip. We talked for a moment before she said, "So when do we start dating?"

"How about now," I replied.

We were matching each other, vying for who could be more easygoing, less afraid of falling in love. It was as if she had stepped from my own personal fantasy. But the initial excitement didn't last more than a few hours. That night, walking back to her apartment, already the insecurities were showing through the cracks. She was a young sadist. She liked making boys cry. She knew I was a masochist from my writing, but she didn't know how to hurt me.

I tell myself I was just getting comfortable when she disappeared last July. But I'm rewriting history, calling up one set of feelings at the expense of another. I remember lying in bed, listening to her talk of revolution. "It never works," I said. "Look at the Communists, Trotsky and the terror famine, Stalin and the twenty-five million. Violence always makes things worse." I was lecturing her idealism. I'm more than ten years older than her and I was telling her to change the system from within. I didn't take her ideas seriously. I imagine a cousin or an aunt patting Vladimir Lenin's cheek, pronouncing confidently he'll grow out of these crazy thoughts. But now I can see the force of Miranda's will. Nothing is more dangerous than someone who is sure they are right.

Back in my neighborhood, Caterina says, "Miranda was in

love with you and you broke her heart. That's all it is." It's Friday; Zeitgeist is packed. Caterina is a fun drunk, full of affection, vivacious. She's here with her boyfriend who is like her—quick to hug people, possessed with an easy laugh. We're all crammed together at picnic tables set in rows in the courtyard. I've always liked crowded places.

"It might be true," I say. I could subscribe to that narrative. The place where the story is supposed to fit is like an abrasion. In the narrative that involves Miranda and me I could be hero or villain. Either would serve as gauze for my feelings. But understanding is not always an option.

Less than a week after the verdict William Du Bois visits Hans at Santa Rita Jail. He enters into the sally port, a small chamber with doors at either end. By design both doors cannot be opened at the same time. He passes through the port, then another locked door, into the interview room. The room is only five by six feet with two chairs and a table. There's an emergency button on the wall. There's no window except for a square of wired plexiglass. When Du Bois is ready to leave he'll ring the bell and the guards will return and accompany him to the exit.

Hans is already there in his red prison fatigues. There's no more need for a suit, no jury to impress. He has his papers with him, a notebook and a pencil. It's just been leaked to the press that Du Bois had negotiated a plea bargain before the trial started, manslaughter with a three-year sentence. The district attorney didn't want the case to go to trial. If Hans had accepted the deal he would be getting out soon. All Hans had to do was produce the body and the body had to be consistent with the crime. But Hans turned him down. Richard Tamor, the assistant defense attorney, filed a sealed notice with the court expressing his opinion that Hans should have accepted the plea bargain. Du Bois did his job before the trial ever started. It was the best deal Hans was ever going to get, but that offer is no longer on the table.

"This is your last chance," he tells Hans. If Hans produces the body and takes responsibility he may someday get out on parole. Du Bois suggests they can return to Paul Hora, it might be possible to get the charge knocked down to murder two, and that maybe Hans would only serve fifteen years.

There's nowhere for Hans to rest his eyes except the linoleum. This is just the jail. After the sentencing Hans will be transferred to San Quentin for evaluation then shipped to another facility like Tehachapi or Lancaster in the Antelope Valley, where the medium-security prisoners live in double and triple bunks crammed into what's supposed to be recreation areas. The short timers—thieves and drug offenders—have no space beyond their mattresses. Maximum-security prisoners, which include all murderers, stay in tiny rooms with a cellmate, released to the yard only two hours a day and often not at all. The California prison system is taxed well past the breaking point thanks to years of negligent governors pandering for votes, and Hans has earned his descent into that particular hell.

"OK," Hans says. He's going to tell him what really happened.

That day, Hans begins, he sat with Nina in the living room trying to convince her to give up legal custody of the children. She began to lose patience and finally said, "Hans, I have to go." She called the children upstairs while Hans was still talking. Cori gave her a hug, wrapping his arms around her and squeezing as hard as he could. When she tried to kiss him he turned his head. Hans and the children watched as Nina ascended the stairs along the side of the house, climbed into her van, and drove away. Then Hans ushered them downstairs where there were computers set up with speakers attached, and they worked educational software and played video games.

Two hours later, at almost six o'clock, the bell rang. It was Nina and she was with Sean. She had forgotten her phone, which had fallen from her purse while she and Hans sat on the couch earlier.

Hans followed her to the couch and then outside. He still wanted to talk about the divorce. Nina got in the driver's seat, Sean next to her, Hans on the curb trying to get Nina to take him seriously. Nina gave Hans a thin smile. She only ever showed her true face to him. "You better give me my money every month, or I'm going to give Cori to Sean to molest," she joked.

According to Hans something rose in Sean, his face contorting into a painful mask. A streak of red flashed against the windshield. Hans says Sean punched Nina, gripping her by the throat, pressing into her tendons. Nina struggled, kicking at the open door, flailing as he crushed her voice box. Hans watched at the side of the van.

Nina lay dead in the driver's seat, her head to one side as if she were resting. Hans says a moment passed. The two spurned lovers had to decide what to do with the body, their animosity dissolving in the face of common cause. Hans gave Sean the keys to the Honda CRX and Sean left and returned with a large duffle bag. They got her body into the bag and filled it with rocks, loading the bag into the passenger seat. Hans told Sean to take the body to Monterey Bay Canyon, three hours south.

The children were still downstairs playing video games. Hans loaded his bicycle into Nina's van and drove the three miles to where it was found near the highway, then bicycled back up the hill. The children were so engrossed in their video games they didn't notice he was gone.

Two days later, the day his mother was supposed to return, Hans found the keys to the CRX slid beneath the door. The hatchback sat in the driveway; the inside of the car was covered in blood.

Hans' confession makes no sense. What about the groceries left in Nina's van? If Nina was gone for two hours, wouldn't she drop the groceries at home first? Why would Sean kill Nina in front of Hans? Why would Hans help him? Wouldn't there be a phone call between Hans and Sean to coordinate stories? Why would he return the car full of blood? Why would he keep the car for two days? How could Sean be sure Hans' mother wouldn't return until that evening and find the keys to the CRX before Hans? And why would Hans cover for Sean, whom he despises?

If anything, the situation Hans described would be perfect for him. Nina would be dead and Sean would end up in jail and Hans would be a free man. Hans' disgust for Sean was palpable during his testimony from the stand, and in fact Hans was the one to accuse Sean of child molestation, reporting him to the police not long after Nina left Hans in 2004.

It's a lie, but somewhere there must be truth. Hans had talked to his lawyers before about Nina leaving and coming back. It's something that never came out in the trial. The submarine canyon in Monterey Bay exists, the only underwater canyon in North America that reaches the shore. In Carmel, south of Santa Cruz, it's possible to cross a berm of pebbles at night carrying one hundred pounds, wade into the water, and drop a duffle bag into a drop-off thirty meters. The currents could rush the package into the canyon's heart, nine thousand feet deep at its center. And there's another point, Moss Landing in Monterey, where Hans could carry Nina from his car to the edge of the landing and drop her several meters into the mouth of the canyon. If the current pulled her into the main trench she would disappear forever.

Du Bois asks Hans why he didn't tell anybody this story before. Why protect Sean? Hans responds, "Because I didn't think anybody should have to go to jail for killing Nina."

Hans' confession is the third false confession to enter my life. Everybody wants to confess to crimes they didn't commit and get their moment in the spotlight where they can tell the "true" story of their victimization. The confessions can't be disproved, not fully. What portion of each tale is true and how much of what they're saying does each of them believe? The truth and the lie combine to create history, like red and yellow paint mixing to orange, the original colors ceasing to exist.

After the verdict I try to contact Sean, but he won't return my letters or calls. One day a yellow envelope arrives with no return address. Inside is a four-gigabyte thumb drive containing thirty hours of audio recordings. They include the entire investigation into Sean: all of his communications with the police and district attorney, various pastors, his pastor's wife, his mother, his mother's boyfriend, friends, and others who came through the house he grew up in who he claims molested him.

The interviews begin April 12, 2007, and end April 26, 2007, almost a week before I first heard of Sean's confession. In the recordings Sean alludes to several people he may have killed: a violent man who lived with his mother for many years, several scout leaders. But Hora and his inspectors track these people down and when Hora confronts Sean in the next interview he claims not to have taken credit for murdering those men. Sean speaks in inferences. He wants people to believe things and doesn't understand implication as a form of lying. There's only one story that keeps coming up in the interviews with Sean and also in the interviews with Sean's pastors. The "half" he was talking about when he said he killed eight and a half people. The one he didn't know was alive or dead.

It was his first victim. Sean was eight or nine years old (he changes his age in separate interviews). He was on a camping trip somewhere near the Mexican border, possibly over the border, possibly in Arizona. He was with his mother and her boyfriend and a number of others who lived in their house or frequently came around. They arrived at the campground in a caravan.

There were many adults, including a man who Sean claims regularly tortured and molested him, and the man's daughter, who was around Sean's age. "She used to braid my hair to my ankles and stick stuff in my ass," Sean says. "She said she took part of my soul."

He came upon her in a shallow pool half a mile from the campground near a waterfall. She had been set upon by a wild animal, or she had fallen and dashed against the rocks. "It was dark," Sean says, his voice lowering. "Darkness is your friend. I was approaching the river. At first I thought I heard an animal cry. It was her. Looking at her in the pond, her face was messed up, arms, chest, her short-cut jeans were ripped. I'm not sure if she was still alive or if it was just that she looked like she looked at me. I got really angry. She wanted me to help her, after what she had done to me. I took back my soul. She was covered in blood; I made her more bloody. And I was liberal about it. I took part of her flesh. I was hungry. I was always hungry then. I drank her blood. She came from the water. My name is Sturgeon. I thought of her as a gift." He waited in the bushes to see what would happen. He saw the father lift the child, wailing with grief. "I knew they would come looking for us. I didn't understand the changes that were happening, that I had gained power, that I could fight back."

Sean's voice on the recording is incredibly creepy, often slipping into a whisper, and finishing with tears or a harsh, manic laugh. He lectures the officers, "Do not allow those you hunt to know you're there . . . The hunt is sacred." He sounds *too* much like a serial killer, as if he was reading a script. Parts of his confession sound like TV episodes. He says one of his victims belonged to an "extra-legal" organization and when he convinced the organization that one of their members was a molester they gave the man to him.

Sean makes fun of himself, but in a self-aggrandizing way. "I've lost lots of fights. I'm not Bruce Lee." He likes to talk and he's proud of his intellectual capabilities, which are impressive, and he likes Paul, who listens patiently, without judging. He says the father of the girl he may have killed when he was eight came to him in 1995 looking for a good time. He says the man lived for a day and a half.

"I said he could leave. All he had to do was get through me to the door. He didn't leave. I showed him all the things that were done to me and the things I learned. He didn't talk, he only listened and screamed. When I was done he was unrecognizable as a human being. It was like something from a horror movie."

"Was the body ever found?" Hora asks.

"I don't think so," Sean replies. A few minutes later Sean tells Hora, "I have a feeling that if we win the case you might even take me out to sushi."

Sean was interviewed at length three times. On one recording he refers to the girl's father as his second to last murder, on another he refers to him as his last murder. He says 6.5 of the murders were direct retaliation, including that of the girl. At different points in the tape he mentions smashing her in the head with a rock and throwing the rock in the pond. He says he bit her neck. Of all the murders the girl is the only one described with any real detail. When they interviewed Sean's mother, sister, and mother's boyfriend, none of them could remember a child dying on a camping trip, or any accident in the woods.

In the final interview, conducted less than two weeks before I first contacted him, Hora and two inspectors sat with Sean for almost five hours trying to convince him to give them any identifying information. Sean enjoyed sparring with them, insisting his only concern was ending the cycle of violence. He admitted it was unlikely that relatives of his victims would seek revenge by hurting people he cared about, but they might, and that was enough. It was the same reason he gave me for not naming his victims. It's a reason I've never believed.

Nothing linking Sean to an actual murder comes out in the recordings. What does come out is a pattern of violence and abandonment: the mother's boyfriend didn't like people and would beat the children if they were disobedient. His mother confirms the children were molested and admits to leaving the children for years at a time.

"Nobody has to worry about me anymore," Sean told me over a year ago. "The worst I ever do to anyone now is quote scripture at them in bad Aramaic." I believed him. On the tapes, Sean's pastor says Sean came to a place of faith where his sins were washed from him. In the months after Sean confessed his murders to his pastor he became violently ill and took to bed. The pastor told Sean his body was responding to this guilt, that God was trying to get his attention. Sean's been born again, turned to Jesus for sustenance, laid his own soul upon the cross. But that's just who he is now. This is America. We reinvent ourselves here all the time.

"We both believe in justice," Sean told Hora at the end of his last interview. "I'll just leave it at that."

Three months after the verdict Sean writes to say he's ready to meet. I arrive at the diner where me met a year ago. It's Friday night.

He walks in with a woman dressed in a white scoop-neck T-shirt and tight jeans. Her hair is dyed blond with black roots, her nails are pressed on and painted white at the tips. A larger black woman is already waiting for him and they sit with her at a table near the door where I join them.

"Are you still into bondage?" Sean asks, motioning toward the blond. "Because I think she likes you."

"He showed me your Web site," the blond girl says. "I like your writing. I like that line about a drop of blood in a glass of water."

"I didn't write that line," I say. "That was a quote from somebody else. When did you meet Sean?"

"Today," she says.

A group of black kids enter the diner, one and two at a time.

Some of them bang on the window, waving at the others before coming in. They're in their late teens and early twenties and there are maybe eight of them total. They stop by the table to say hello to Sean. "You must be Elliott," they say, shaking my hand. One kid has gold plating on his front teeth. Another has thick black glasses with no lenses in them. He squeezes my hand hard, stares at me. He might be the youngest of the group, probably only seventeen years old. His glassless glasses remind me of the disguise my father claims to have worn when he killed a man. But the boy's face, both tough and innocent, reminds me of Cateyes. Sean tells them he got good news recently: the police are giving him back his guns.

"Who are these people?" I ask.

"I know people," Sean replies. He looks straight at me, his hands folded on the table, as if we were having a staring contest.

"What do you consider consent?" the black woman next to Sean asks me. "Do you think you have the right to write about people who don't want to be written about?"

"It's complicated," I say. "But if I contact someone and tell them I want to write about them and they meet with me, I consider that consent."

"He has my consent," Sean says. "I told him he could write about me in an email." He smiles as if he has nothing to do with this. As if he was as surprised by the question as I was and hadn't orchestrated this evening's event. As if we both just walked into some absurdist play together.

Sean unbuttons his shirt. He has two large scars beneath his chest as if he had once had breast implants, and more scars on his stomach. "I've been wasting away," he says. "I'm sick with something. I've lost thirty or forty pounds even though I eat like eight thousand calories a day."

"You look fine," I say.

Sean leaves his shirt open, inviting me to stare at his hairless pink skin and all his marks. "So," he says. "What do you want to know?"

The black woman leaves. I should leave, but I don't. I ask him why he confessed to eight murders and he says Paul Hora asked about them. Hora had heard through Hans somehow. It contradicts earlier statements he made and I tell him that. I ask about the girl he may have murdered, why his mother and her boyfriend can't remember a child dying in the woods. He says they were hippies and they were doing drugs. Also, they don't like talking to the police.

I ask him about the "extra-legal" organization. "What extra-legal organization are you talking about?"

"You want to know the name of the extra-legal organization?"

"Yes. I do."

"Hey guys," Sean calls out. "He wants to know the name of an extra-legal organization." The boys shamble over from their tables and surround me. They take positions behind me and to my right and in front of me behind Sean, all of them talking at once, like a parody of a Greek chorus. It's like the group homes all over again. I feel something resembling fear but I've been afraid so many times I'm used to it.

One kid says, "What do you mean by that? What's extra-legal?"

"That's what I'm trying to find out. That's what I'm asking."

"Talk to me," another says. "Look at me. What are you talking about? Make me understand."

"You heard of Chauncey Bailey?" one of the kids behind Sean says. "He got killed because he was trying to report shit he wasn't supposed to."

"Are you threatening me?" I ask. "Are you trying to intimidate me?"

"Why do you keep writing stuff down?" the girl sitting next to me asks, letting out a lazy laugh and leaning her shoulder toward my shoulder.

"Hey," Sean says. "We don't want to surround him and be threatening." The boys move noisily back to their tables by the windows. Sean starts speaking in a low, menacing voice, squinting, almost spitting. He talks about Nina, the pain he carries. Asks me if I know what he's been through as a result of things Josh and I have written about him. He says people stalk him. Accost him near his home.

"I doubt it," I say. "I haven't published anything about you yet."

Sean says he doesn't believe me. The girl presses her leg against my leg and I move away from her. "Am I making you uncomfortable?" she says. "Why do you keep moving away from me?"

"Everybody gather around," Sean says. "I want everybody to hear this." He's speaking really loudly. He wants the entire restaurant to hear him. The boys come over again. "I hereby withdraw my consent for this story to be told. I remove consent. You do not have consent to write about me."

"You don't have a person's consent, you can't do it," the blond girl says.

"I got it on tape," one of the kids says, waving a small black tape recorder. "You don't have consent."

After seeing Sean I go to a friend's house, the same woman I kissed whom I met at the conference in Portland last August. She's packing her things, preparing to go to the Democratic National Convention. It's almost two in the morning and I lie on her couch, too angry to sleep.

"He set me up to be intimidated," I say. "It was ridiculous."

"You can stay here," she says. She means in the living room.

I don't stay though. I go home.

Sean changed his mind about being written about. I told him several times he wouldn't like how I portrayed him. Maybe he was just realizing what that meant: not that I would show both his good and bad sides, but that I would show a version of him he wouldn't recognize, someone that had little in common with how he saw himself. It was too much control to give away. He wanted to tell his own story. In an interview with *48 Hours* soon after our meeting, he admits he made the whole thing up. He says he was at least partly responsible for one death, maybe more. He says he pulled the number "eight and a half" out of thin air because he didn't want to testify.

"Did you confess to killing eight and a half people to try and help Hans?" the interviewer asks.

"I can't answer that question," Sean says. And I wonder if he can't answer because he doesn't want to incriminate himself or because he really doesn't know.

During the trial people frequently asked how a person like Nina could be with men like Hans and Sean. It struck me as a ridiculous question. Sean loved Nina and Hans wasn't capable of love. Sean gave her a bridge from the world Hans trapped her in. A little over a year ago he extended a bloody hand to help me across my own chasm and into the next place I would go in my life, the woods where I would continue my search. I didn't know Sean would push me toward myself. This book is not about him.

In a powerfully written article, an author tells the story of his years on Ritalin, a methylamphetamine compound indistinguishable from Adderall. The first time he took Ritalin, he wrote, he felt a surge of artificial illumination so sharp it made him grin. But by the end of the piece he had seen the error of his ways, come face-to-face with the economy of decreasing rewards. He decided he had had enough concentration and intensity and missed the person he used to be, someone who was more curious and lazy than the piercingly focused person he'd become. When I met the author in January of this year and told him I was working on a book called *The Adderall Diaries,* he asked if I had any. I said I thought he had quit. "Well," he explained, waving his hand, "I've made a separate peace. I still take it, just not as often. After all, I've got to work." It was almost midnight and we were at a party thrown by a mutual friend and he was ready to pop a pill that would keep him up through the morning.

In that same article the author calls Ritalin as euphoria inducing as any illegal drug he had ever tried. In fact, he said, the effects were better. And compared to street drugs, it was cheap. He sounded like the Beatniks, William Burroughs and Joan Vollmer, cracking inhalers, soaking the amphetamine sheets in their coffee, or popping amphetamine and meta-amphetamine tablets, sometimes taking more than a hundred milligrams at a time. Jack Kerouac cranked out one hundred twenty feet of single-spaced, Benzedrine-induced prose in less than three weeks, producing *On the Road,* his greatest novel. The book defined the exuberance and promise of a generation, but it's actually a story of children scrambling across the continent strung out on speed.

For now I've stopped snorting Adderall and cut down to fifteen milligrams a day. Far less than the Beatniks or any of the addicts on the ADHD online discussion boards typing in all caps, begging for help. Some days I take only five milligrams, or none at all. I don't take any more sleeping pills and I don't take antidepressants. It's not perfect. It's not like Robert Pirsig's sense of well being at the end of *Zen and the Art of Motorcycle Maintenance,* but Pirsig allowed himself to come to false conclusions. Things were not going to be OK as we learned in his only other book, *Lila,* published seventeen years later.

When I was sixteen and decided to quit drugs and graduate high school, I read *Zen and the Art of Motorcycle Maintenance* seven times. I would finish the book and start over again. I didn't understand what Pirsig was saying, but I was hooked on his sense of resolution. The final lines of the book conclude, *"We've won it. It's going to get better now. You can sort of tell these things."* It made me feel good. In the poems I wrote constantly I tried for a similar thing, an epiphany to wrap things with a neat little bow. I searched for that in each of my novels, but kept coming to the same conclusion. In every book I ever wrote the point was to do as much as you could after coming to terms with your limitations. I can't wake up one day with a healthy relationship with my mother and father and a sense of abundance. I wake up instead and I think my father hates me, and I know that I am partly to blame. I've written about him and made him into a villain. I've made him unhappy. I've mythologized myself and withheld my love, pretended my actions were justified by his actions. I put that on with my clothes and wear it throughout the day.

Pirsig's conclusion was too much, too sweeping. It couldn't possibly be true. Of course things wouldn't be OK. They would be better sometimes and worse others. In her memoir *Fierce Attachments,* Vivian Gornick meets an old friend who tells her about a boy she grew up with and how well he turned out. *"Who would have thought my brother would turn out spiritual,"* the friend said. She could just as easily have been describing Sean, who came from a world without structure and found it inside the comforting walls of his church. *"Oh Dorothy,"* Vivian replied. *"Davey's not spiritual. He's looking for a way to put his life together, and he's got no equipment with which to do it. So he turned religious. It's a mark of how lost he is, not how found he is, that he's a rabbi in Jerusalem."*

When I was sixteen I didn't need Gornick, I needed simplicity. I needed a promise and a path. I needed to know that from now on, things were going to get better. I had been getting high since I was ten, running away since I was thirteen. I found what I needed in the consumption and creation of art, though I didn't see it that way at the time. I stopped getting high. I graduated high school in two years. I went to college. But it didn't hold because there are no permanent solutions. I got out of college and I started getting high again. And I became a stripper. And I had an overdose and I went to graduate school and I drifted and traveled and I saw the world and I surprised myself with the things I could and couldn't do. I saw peace and war and prosperity and things got better and they got worse, sometimes at the same time. There is no clear path. I have two models: my mother and my father, sickness and chaos. My mother long-suffering, the victim, my father a naked peacock strutting through the rooms, colorful, aggressive. I hear doors open but can't always see them. I move forward without a path. I am not sad all the time but I will always be sad sometimes. I can't read Pirsig anymore. Neat conclusions do nothing for me. I write to make sense, to communicate, to connect. I rely on people like Gornick to guide me through, people who keep searching when everything is dark. The search is the meaning. Even when her book ends.

Because we are silent the noise of the street is more compelling. It reminds me that we are not in the Bronx, we are in Manhattan: the journey has been more than a series of subway stops for each of us. Yet tonight this room is so like that other room, and the light, the failing summer light, suddenly it seems a blurred version of that other pale light, the one falling on us in the foyer.

My mother breaks the silence. In a voice remarkably free of emotion—a voice detached, curious, only wanting information— she says to me, "Why don't you go already? Why don't you walk away from my life? I'm not stopping you."

I see the light, I hear the street. I'm half in, half out.

"I know you're not, Ma."

I need to see my father.

I have four books by my father. They sit next to mine on the middle shelf on my bookcase. In each the author bio changes, as if it were written by a different person. An early novel, published when he was around twenty-six, says he graduated from the University of Natal, served as airborne meteorologist with the South African Air Force, and worked as a geologist for two years before immigrating to the United States. His first hard-cover book, released when he was living with his parents, has a picture of him in a jacket and tie, smoking a pipe, and says the author lives in Chicago when he is not on assignments overseas. It also says he is currently completing another book in his Florida home. The book he was "completing in his Florida home" is the book he wrote on his parents' sunporch, with children lighting firecrackers in the park across the street. That book says he's a former TV producer. His last book, based on the life of Jesus Christ, says he studied the life and teachings of Jesus at the North Park Theological Seminary in Chicago, and that a play he wrote based on his son's novel will soon be a film.

I'm not sure if he changed his biographies because he thought it would help sell books, or because he thought it would be funny, or if he really wanted to be someone else. Perhaps he recognized reality as constructed and wasn't willing to let anyone else build it for him. What we've really been fighting about all these years is authorship.

It's a beautiful summer day in Chicago and chairs are set up on the edge of the sidewalk. My father arrives wearing a do-rag dec-orated with skull and crossbones, a ring with the face of a demon on his finger, a rubber brace wrapped around his other hand. The fingers on the hand with the brace are curled painfully. He wears a thick leather strap two inches wide buckled around each wrist; one contains a watch, the other something else, both with skull and crossbones on top. He wears a leather vest over a long sleeve denim shirt. The vest is open and the shirt is unbuttoned almost to his navel. He's limping terrifically as he enters the café, grip-ping the counters. I ask him to meet me at one of the tables out-side. I'll get us something.

This used to be a rougher area but now there are restaurants and even a gym. We're near Loyola University. The school has been expanding south while Andersonville, formerly known as Edgewater, and the trendy bars there gradually spread north to meet it. Two stops away, in Rogers Park, things are also cleaning up, though not as dramatically. The crackheads aren't hanging out in front of the station as much, and the bar next to the train has finally taken the boards off the windows.

"So how's the sadomasochism?" my father jokes, as I sit across from him. "Got any women beating you up these days?"

"There's one," I say, placing two coffees in front of us.

Ladies pass on their way to Sheridan and the lake. He says hello to every woman who walks by. He's always done that. When I was younger it made me uncomfortable. But now that he's over seventy it seems harmless. "That one looks like she'll dominate you," he says, pointing to a tall, dark woman in platforms and a summer dress.

"Dominant women rarely look dominant," I tell him. "You would never be able to pick one in a crowd." I try to explain why that might be, but he's not interested. He just nods and smiles.

It's three in the afternoon and hot. I feel uncomfortable and not sure of what to say. It seems like I should have been prepared with a plan. I thought if I just kept my heart open everything would be OK. But the truth is my heart is not as open as I want it to be.

The conversation moves forward in fits and starts. He tells me when my mother was dying he was so confused he couldn't stop screaming. He says I can't resent that person because that person is not who he is now; that person no longer exists.

"When you ran away I had aches all over my body and I couldn't sleep. I tried traveling but it didn't help. I suffered much more than you did." I tell him I don't get any pleasure out of his suffering. I don't want anything to do with his suffering. He says, "I made a lot of mistakes when you were younger. I should have been more strict." He complains about the social workers, how they only took my side and didn't even ask his opinion. He talks about a profile on me that ran in the *Tribune*.[21] He refers to it as an article about him, which it wasn't. The reporter contacted my father. He sent her over fifty emails and she hardly used any of it. She quoted my father telling her that I was a "bad seed" and "human garbage." She wrote that I was damaged, which my father found offensive. He wrote a letter to the editor saying his son wasn't damaged; his son was a successful author.

"She had an agenda, that fucking cunt," he says. "I would break every bone in her body."

"I thought she went easy on you," I reply. I tell him we have different memories and interpretations of those memories and that's unlikely to change. I feel like this isn't going well. My father never wanted a third party involved when I was sleeping on the streets. He didn't accept the authority of the court. He says the social workers would make appointments and cancel them at the last minute. He stopped fighting the state for custody of me because the hearings kept being continued.

"You have to understand," he says. "I was a working stiff. I had to make a living. Me and your stepmother were just trying to get by." He tells me his neighbors think he's a child abuser because of things they read about me. He says he took down the most recent reviews he left of my books on Amazon but I tell him I'd rather he left them up. Once I've read them it doesn't matter whether they're up or down; I've already integrated his words into my life. I tell him I keep screen shots of all of them so I won't think I'm going crazy when they disappear. I wish every action was recorded and we could have a little Google bar to search ourselves, find out what we said last time and in response to what.

"I'm always going to retaliate," he says.

---

21. Ellen Warren, *Chicago Tribune*, March 18, 2005.

"We all think we're retaliating," I say. "That's the nature of conflict. We all think our actions are justified by someone else's actions. But actually, we're responsible for what we do."

"No," he says. "That's not how it is. You hit me I'll hit you back."

I want to laugh. My father is pure Chicago and I'm turning into some new age San Franciscan full of self-help platitudes. If Chicago ever attacked San Francisco it would be like the Nazis invading Belgium. He talks about all the women he's seeing, the women he meets online, rich women with houses all over the world. One he meets in Florida every winter. But how he always comes home to my stepmother and what a wonderful woman she is. I never really got to know my stepmother, and I resented her for a long time, but that had nothing to do with her. That was about me and my father and my mother. She was always nice to me, and a good mom to my little brother and sister. My little brother and sister turned out fine.

"You never know what matters," my father says. "Everything important comes from left field."

I tell him I'm writing a memoir that was supposed to be a true crime book and that in the process of writing it I realized that I love him and my relationship with him is the most important relationship in my life. He looks at me like maybe I'm pulling his leg.

After sitting outside for an hour, he asks if I need to go somewhere.

"No," I say. "Not for a while."

He offers to help with my memoir; he probably remembers things better than I do. I tell him he doesn't even remember how many high schools I went to. And anyway, the memories are the point. What we remember, and how we order and interpret what we believe to be true, are what shapes who we are. I tell him the book is for me. My books are not letters to him. He says I should write whatever I want and promises he won't read it. I tell him I appreciate that, but I don't really believe him.

"I read your memoir," I say. "I read about the guy beating you up in front of your parents' house."

"Oh yeah," he says. "That's hard to think about. Even now. I was traumatized. You don't know what it's like to take a beating like that. They got the jump on me. Hit me with a club." I ask about the pictures and he confirms there were pictures of him with black eyes and blood all over his shirt, but he doesn't know what he did with them. For a while he kept them as evidence.

It's Memorial Day and they're closing the café early so I ask if he would like to go to the beach, which is only a block away. We walk past his car, a new silver Cadillac convertible. He says his wife drives a Hyundai. He says Hyundais are great cars, which sounds funny and also comforting coming from him. I remember all his giant, beautiful American cars, the black '74 Oldsmobile with white and black striped interior, the '70 Cougar, cars big enough to take up the entire road. My fondest memory of my father is when he let me drive the Cougar with the top down in the parking lot at Warren State Park, maneuvering that beast past all the parked cars, with its gleaming sky blue paint job and white leather seats, the hood angled above its muscular engine. I tell him my friends stole his car.

"Which one?" he asks.

"I don't know."

My father walks awkwardly, body bent close to the ground, swinging his feet forward from his knees, like a puppet. He looks like he's going to fall with every step and I stay close, ready to catch him. I wish we had worked things out before, negotiated our lies and truths so our histories could be a shared one. But that's not how things work, at least not between us. We were too stubborn then and we're just as stubborn now. Our memories are calcified. Halfway down the street he leans against a pole, breathing heavily. I can't believe how he has deteriorated in five years. At the same time, he's sharp as ever. He hasn't lost any of his intellect. His face is heavily lined with wrinkles, but handsome, more handsome than I remember. The contrast is hard to read. It's as if he were dying and vibrantly alive at the same time. He appears so healthy he'll live forever, even as his body collapses beneath him.

"Do I seem worse?" he asks.

"Only a little," I say.

We sit for another hour at the lake drinking lemonade. I don't know what it's in response to but I tell my father, "I'm straight-forward. I'm an honest person."

"You?" he says, laughing like it's the funniest thing he ever heard. "Sure you are." Before we met I thought I had created a way for us to see that our memories were equally valid. I don't know how to spend time with someone who thinks I'm a liar. We both think we're indulging each other. We both think we're doing one another a favor by pretending to forget. He says he goes dancing on Friday nights with his wife. I guess it doesn't matter if you're crippled if you have good rhythm. He asks if I would go with them.

"I've never seen you dance," he says. "I hear you're a good dancer."

"I am," I say. "I'm a good dancer."

It's getting late in the day. I've been with my father over three hours. I'm meeting my sister for dinner soon. He asks if I would like a ride but I say I'd rather walk.

There's a woman nearby with a book open on her lap, a bunch of children playing in a foam-padded park, a homeless guy sleeping on a bench. It could be any hot day in Chicago. What did I want? What did I expect? I had told myself he couldn't give me anything, but I must have wanted something because I feel disappointed.

"You know, in your memoir you say you killed that guy that beat you up."

"I did? I wrote that?" He stiffens, not smiling at all.

"Yeah. You did."

"Wow. I can't believe I wrote that."

"But you didn't. I looked into it. There wasn't any murder like that that year."

"With a shotgun?"

"Yeah. I went through all the papers. I even found a study."

"But you don't have his name." It's almost a question. He doesn't remember exactly what he wrote and he gave me the only copy. I agree with him. I don't have the man's name, and without his name I can't prove he wasn't murdered in 1971, less than six months before I was born. And I can't find the man's son, which is what I really want. When I first read the memoir I had been certain it happened. I've been wrong about him so many times and I wanted to be wrong about this. I looked for assault records from 1970, when the beating occurred, but they've all been purged. I've thought of asking about this murder many times. But I had decided not to ask him about it today. I thought we had more important things to talk about, and I didn't want to push him away. I wanted to suck some of the poison out of our relationship. And then I asked him anyway, and now we're at the lake and he's insinuating the murder is true. But I don't want it to be true. That would make me the second child orphaned by my father.

My father grins like a boy playing a prank. All that water spread out before us, the condo towers on either side of us, the tan brick public buildings behind us. Chicago is a sturdy city. It's possible I know less now than I knew before. I watch my father's face, the area where the tangle of wrinkles fade into where he wore a beard for many years and his skin is smooth. The sun is full on us.

"Maybe it didn't happen then," he says. Though he clearly wants me to think that it did. But do I? This is my father.

EPILOGUE

On July 7, 2008, two days before he's scheduled for sentencing, Hans Reiser leads the police to Nina's remains. He takes them through the woods near his house to a thin deer path that cuts sharply off the trail, then sits for a moment in the dirt. He's handcuffed to William Du Bois and accompanied by a team of SWAT officers. Helicopters hover overhead. "If you dig there," he says, pointing to an end of turned earth, "you'll find her feet."

I had visited him in the jail just five days earlier. It was our first and only meeting. We spoke over a phone line, staring at each other through bulletproof glass. He told me he recognized me from court. He said he hadn't received a fair trial and asked me to investigate witnesses against him. He said he would be very impressed if I could find out a few things. He didn't show any remorse; he was angry about how he had been treated. I said, "Who cares if you received a fair trial if you're guilty of murder?"

"You can believe whatever you want to believe," he said, hanging up the phone. But with his sentencing approaching he finally gave in.

In late August Hans gives Paul Hora his recorded confession. He says on September 3, 2006, in a fit of rage, he punched Nina in the face, then choked her. He says he placed her in a duffel bag and stored her for two days in the back of the Honda CRX while he went out at night with a small shovel and dug the hole. He dug the grave at a plateau three hundred feet below a hiking trail. The hole is four feet deep at the end and four feet long in hard, packed ground.

The confession is itself a lie. The murder was premeditated. Sources tell me that prior to giving Hora his statement Hans admitted to digging Nina's grave two weeks in advance.

On August 29, 2008, Judge Goodman approves the bargain negotiated by Hora. In exchange for leading the police to Nina's body, confessing, and waiving his right to appeal, the charge is reduced from murder one to murder two with a mandatory sentence of fifteen to life. It's not a significant reduction. Unless the California Department of Corrections changes dramatically Hans is unlikely ever to be released from prison. Nina's remains are shipped to Russia so her family can give her a proper burial and begin the process of mourning.

Many think that, despite waiving his right to appeal, Hans will find a way to continue his case. "As long as Hans Reiser is alive," Assistant Defense Attorney Richard Tamor says, "this story will never end."

STEPHEN ELLIOTT is the author of seven books including *Happy Baby*, a finalist for the New York Public Library's Young Lions Award, as well as a Best Book of 2004 in Salon.com, *Newsday*, *Chicago New City*, the *Journal News*, and the *Village Voice*.

Elliott's writing has been featured in *Esquire*, the *New York Times*, *GQ*, *The Best American Nonrequired Reading 2005 and 2007*, *The Best American Erotica 2006*, and *Best Sex Writing 2006*.

In January 2009 he launched TheRumpus.net, a daily online culture magazine.

The Adderall Diaries has been set in Utopia. Book design by Rachel Holscher. Composition by BookMobile Design and Publishing Services, Minneapolis, Minnesota. Manufactured by Friesens on acid-free paper.